stin

a biography

robert sellers

Omnibus Press
london / new york / sydney / cologne

784
SELLERS
1

Edited by Chris Charlesworth
Art Direction by Mike Bell
Book Designed by AB3 Design
Picture Research by Debbie Dorman
Project and typesetting co-ordinated by Caroline Watson

ISBN 0.7119.2107.5
Order No: OP45764

Exclusive distributors:

Book Sales Limited,
8/9 Frith Street,
London W1V 5TZ, UK.

Music Sales Corporation,
225 Park Avenue South,
New York, NY 10003, USA.

Music Sales Pty Limited,
120 Rothschild Avenue,
Rosebery, NSW 2018, Australia.

To the Music Trade only:
Music Sales Limited,
8/9 Frith Street,
London W1V 5TZ, UK.

A 8 11 90

Typeset by Saxon Printing Limited, Derby.
Printed in Great Britain by St Edmundsbury Press Limited,
Bury St Edmunds, Suffolk.

CONTENTS

CHAPTER ONE

JUST ANOTHER BEGINNING . . .

"I feel I'm a bit of an upstart. I live in North London, but it's a pretence. I'm really from Wallsend On Tyne and was brought up in a back to back place near the shipyard. I feel as if I got here by the most subtle trickery imaginable."

ONE GLOOMY late January morning in 1977 Sting, his wife of nine months actress Frances Tomelty, their six-week-old son Joe and the family dog all headed for London in a battered Citröen Dyane loaded with everything they owned.

"Everybody told me I was crazy. My parents, the headmaster and the people I was working with all said I was mad because I had a wife and kid to support, and I was giving up a salaried career, a pension and a secure niche in life. But I knew I had to make the break or I would have gone mad." They moved in temporarily with an agent friend of his wife's called Pippa Markham, and occupied the living room floor of her one bedroom flat near Battersea. With Sting forced to go on the dole it was a difficult and stressful beginning.

"We used to look at Joe lying on the makeshift bed on the floor," said Frances, "look at each other and think, what have we done? But Sting is a determined bread winner and I knew we'd never starve." "It sounds dramatic," he says. "And it was, my life just changed overnight."

He was born Gordon Matthew Sumner on October 2, 1951 in Wallsend, Northumberland, a working class industrial district of Newcastle. "I was raised Catholic, and in the rock world which is hedonistic it sets you apart to have had an upbringing that was rooted in magic and religion. I'm not a devout Catholic but I'm not sure I've broken away from it. All that was inculcated into my brain as a child, that there is a heaven and hell and sin, is inside my psyche and will never come out.''

Sting was the eldest of four children, with a brother Philip and two sisters Angela and Anita. Their father was an engineer who later became a milkman, their mother a hairdresser. "I suppose that part of my egocentric drive is an attempt to transcend my background. I've rejected it as something I don't want to be like. I grew up with a pretty poor family life in a working class area and the whole thing for me was escape.''

The Sumner family lived in a terraced house close to the river Tyne, and the primary image of Sting's childhood was of a shipyard at the bottom of his street which every year built a single tanker that after 12 months vanished into the sea.

Stewart Copeland has contested this romantic image, however. "Sting likes to imagine himself as coming from a shipyard in Newcastle, he talks about what a hole it was. But actually his parents' house is a nice suburban home," he said in 1981 and this may well be nearer the truth for Sting has since deliberated on the theme of myth making. "Why be absolutely truthful, we're in the business of creating myth, does it have to be actual fact. I could make my past more glamorous, I haven't done a lot of it but it goes on."

Sting did not enjoy a happy childhood. "It wasn't unusually bad it's just that I have a certain mentality that made childhood very painful," he recalls. "I remember just aching, real heartache. It wasn't my parents' fault, it's just the way my brain was working.

But at an early age he realised the importance of having an education. "Where I was brought up nothing much was expected of you. I think I was very bright as a kid and I knew there was an escape route and it was through working well at school, it was through reading books. An intellectual interest has always been with me. I read *Treasure Island* when I was six."

After passing his 11-plus Sting attended St. Cuthbert's, Catholic grammar school. This move only served to alienate him from his contemporaries who mostly continued along the secondary school treadmill, and Sting found himself with few friends. Even today he admits to only a handful of true companions.

His education at St. Cuthbert's was rather reactionary. "I was taught by priests and spent my entire educational life with this crucifix of a tortured man bleeding everywhere." It was at grammar school that he began to develop a rebellious and independent streak but his natural broadening of character had its pitfalls. "We'd be sent to Father Walsh for six of the best. It was the most cruel, humiliating punishment ever. After four strokes of the cane you were crying. We were caned for very trivial things, like arguing. I was caned a lot at school."

It was during this period that Sting developed his interest in music. An uncle emigrated to Canada leaving behind a guitar, which he learnt to play by strumming along to Beatles' and Rolling Stones' records. In his fourth year at school, and in an unbridled attempt to be hip, he began listening to obscure jazz recordings by the likes of Charlie Mingus and Thelonious Monk. At first he didn't take to them, "but I persevered because I thought they were doing me good. It was like having to take some kind of medicine." He soon became fascinated with the sound, particularly jazz bass and it was probably for this reason, and the fact that his hero Paul McCartney played the instrument, that he took up the bass guitar himself. In 1969 Sting left school with 'A' levels in Economics, Geography and English. He entered Warwick University but left after only a term, because he felt it was as restrictive as school had been. Returning to Newcastle he had a succession of menial jobs, working on a building site for six months and later in the Civil Service from which he was almost sacked for taking four-hour lunch breaks. More positive was his enrolment in teachers' training college where he studied for a teachers' certificate in music and English, even though the decision came mainly from a feeling of not knowing what else to do.

While at college Sting's music developed in earnest. He started to frequent local jazz clubs, particularly The Wheatsheaf where he sometimes stood in for the bass player of the resident band The Phoenix Jazzmen. One night he failed to show up altogether and Sting plugged in his electric bass to cover for the entire set. It was the Jazzmen's trombonist who gave Sting his unusual name because in the striped jumper he wore he resembled a bee.

It wasn't long before he had fashioned a reputation for himself among the Newcastle jazz fraternity as a musician of consummate talent. He was asked to join The Riverside Men, the top trad jazz band in the area, and later The Newcastle Big Band.

"I was conscious that there was some sort of apprenticeship being served. I learned to read music and worked hard practising every day. I was still a student at training college but I was earning a fortune every night. I had a new car and was definitely the face of the college," he recalled later. By the time Sting joined them in 1970 The Big Band had already amassed sizeable local fame and Sting performed abroad with them at The San

Sebastian Festival in 1970 and 1972. A limited edition live album emerged from this period and Sting continued to play with The Band until their split in 1976.

In 1972 Sting formed his own group, Last Exit. The name referred to the motorway turn off for Newcastle, but could also have been derived from the Hubert Selby Jnr novel *Last Exit To Brooklyn*. Beginning in small venues, the band developed a fair following and went on to play in Spain, on a cruise, and to release a single and a limited nine-track cassette LP.

IT **WAS AROUND** the middle seventies that Sting began singing and writing songs. "The fact that I can sing is an accident of genetics," he once said. He often listened to Cleo Laine and Flora Purim, female singers who like him vocalized on a high scale. "I had a naturally high voice and I tried to model myself on them. I never tried to disguise the high voice and never felt embarrassed by it."

In 1974 Sting completed his three-year training course and took a teaching post at a primary school in Cramlington, a mining community eight miles from Newcastle. Although during his training he had taught secondary school teenagers, St. Paul's Catholic First School offered the more difficult task of tutoring nine and 10-year-olds. Sting voices doubts today that they learnt much from him, but believes those days were instrumental in teaching him how to control and present himself in front of large groups of people.

In December 1974 Last Exit were booked as the backing band for a musical rock nativity play with a young Irish actress called Frances Tomelty playing The Virgin Mary. It wasn't long before Sting and Frances were seeing each other on a regular basis. "He would come round to my flat and I'd cook him cheese on toast while he sat and played me the songs he'd written," she said.

Sting even visited her parents in Andersontown, Belfast Catholic Country, but felt so uneasy about being English there that he allegedly feigned an Irish accent in public. The couple married on May 1 1976.

"He was the reason we got married of course," Sting joked in a *NME* interview, pointing to his son Joe, who was born on 23 November, 1976. "The constitution we set our marriage on was very flexible. We would have this kid but I didn't ever want to say I gave up the best years of my life for him, because it was said to me."

By July 1976 Sting had left his teaching post and gone on the dole. He realised that if he wanted to pursue a full-time musical career he would have to concentrate on it one hundred per cent. Secure in their home town success Last Exit now made a reconnaissance trip to London, playing concerts and hoping to land a record deal. Though nothing was forthcoming and the band returned to Newcastle, Sting managed to attract the attention of Virgin Music who shrewdly snapped up the publishing rights to his material. "It wasn't a good deal but I was so excited I took it. I thought, I'm a real songwriter now, I could talk to people about my publishers, it was a great thrill." However, the eventual repercussions of this contract would lead Sting and Virgin boss Richard Branson into a high court confrontation.

One of Last Exit's few December gigs of 1976 was at the local Polytechnic and was attended by a drummer called Stewart Copeland, in the area with his own group Curved Air. Unimpressed with the band, Copeland was however immediately aware of Sting's star potential. "He had then what he has now," said the drummer. "This fantastic presence."

Copeland's admiration had much to do with Sting's decision to move his family down to London where he found himself rehearsing almost straight away in a small room at Stewart's Mayfair flat. "I was quite impressed," said Sting, "until I found out later he had been squatting there."

The first crude model of The Police, a name chosen by Stewart to tie in with his family's law enforcement connections (and the logic that every time the police service was mentioned in the media it would serve as a reminder of the band) also included Henri Padovani whose inadequacy on guitar is now legendary early Police folklore.

The brainchild of Stewart Copeland, The Police were the antithesis of Curved Air, who were, like many of their contemporaries, always in debt with record companies, due mainly to preposterously high advances they could never hope to repay. Copeland's tack with The Police was to create a band devoid of record company support. His plans had added credence due to the anti-establishment fervour of the new punk movement, which excited both Sting and himself so much. But The Police would never be accepted into the élitist circles of punkdom. The music press were cynical about their musical heritage and the overall feeling in the punk community, especially after the arrival of Andy Summers, was that they were too credible, too old and musically too proficient.

"We were too young to have been in Woodstock, but too old to be punks," Sting said in 1979. But they were still seen as punk bandwagon jumpers, especially when they supported Cherry Vanilla on tour and played at a French punk festival which also featured The Clash, The Jam and others. Sting would answer the critics by saying that all The Police shared with punks was their raw energy.

"In 1977 we got in through the back door," he

said. "We weren't the real thing, Andy's age gave us away. But the revolution was upon us and you had to pick sides. I wasn't into the Genesis type thing and although at first I didn't like The Pistols' music, the attitude was so compelling I had to side with them." Looking back on those early days Sting told *The Face* in 1985: "We used the movement as a flag of convenience. I really got off on this drive to destroy the music industry which had been trying to keep me out for years."

Indeed Sting openly disliked punk music, a feeling that led to his classic comment at an early Police gig when he said, "All right we're going to play some punk now which means the lyrics are banal and the music is terrible." The audience, all punks were not amused. "He totally blew it," recalls Stewart.

The Police's musical output in 1977 stemmed directly from Copeland, and though Sting was less than impressed with his ideas the energy of the man kept him interested. He did nearly leave in March to play bass on a Billy Ocean tour but was persuaded against it. On February 12 The Police were at Pathway studios recording their first single 'Fall Out' at a cost of £150. It was released in May on Illegal Records, Stewart's own label, and sold well among the punk fraternity. It eventually sold in excess of 100,000 copies when re-issued in December 1979.

But Sting confessed that the leap from playing jazz in Newcastle to being on the fringe of the London punk and new wave scene had been a difficult one. "I thought that as I was new and unknown I'd give it a go. It was a new experience. I didn't have much to offer apart from singing ability and being able to play bass, so I just went along with it. But as time went on I found that I wanted to say more, so I started writing. But one problem I kept coming up against was the limitations of our guitarist."

Within a month of the release of 'Fall Out' Andy Summers joined The Police. They became, albeit temporarily, a four-piece, playing their first gig in that format at London's Music Machine on July 25, 1977. The three had already met during session work, which Sting and Stewart sometimes took to supplement their income, and Andy was invited to watch them at a Marquee gig. In fact they had already crossed paths when Andy was playing guitar on Mike Oldfield's Tubular Bells Tour at which Last Exit had been the support on the Newcastle leg. Though not too impressed with their performance at the Marquee in early June, Andy felt that the potential was there.

It was here that Sting began to express dissatisfaction with Henri Padovani's talent as a musician. His technical inadequacy was limiting the group's output and dampening Sting's more adventurous songs. "I would write guitar parts and find that he just couldn't play them," he said. Andy, eager to get into the band, ran into Stewart in Oxford Street one day and demanded there and then to join. He was accepted and this proved a turning point in The Police's history, enabling Sting to become more sophisticated in his writing, safe in the knowledge that Andy could handle anything he wrote. Sting now began to take over the musical direction of the band, Copeland's fast rock songs gave way to Sting's more melodic and hook-lined compositions. Padovani, never happy with the situation left on August 12, only days after a recording session with John Cale of Velvet Underground fame had proved fruitless. The new three-piece premièred at Rebecca's in Birmingham six days after the split.

In September 1977, Laurence Impey, an old school friend of Stewart's, became the group's first manager. This proved a lack-lustre appointment for on the group's return from Germany in

November after playing with Eberhard Schoener, one of Andy's prior commitments before joining The Police, management promises of record contracts and new equipment were not forthcoming. All that greeted them was a drafty rehearsal room, and not a single gig in the pipeline. The Police disappeared off the scene, distilling what little momentum and credibility they had managed to muster by that time. The only positive thing to emerge from this lengthy rehearsal period was that Andy was worked into the group. However, this was hardly solace for an otherwise wasted spell and the trio ultimately walked out on Impey.

"But we still couldn't get gigs," said Sting. "We were in a hole. We had what we thought was a great band, but it was just the wrong time. We decided the only way out of the rut was to make an album." With the money they had made on the 'Fall Out' single and some financial aid from Stewart's brother Miles, The Police secured a studio and a starting date of January 13, 1978.

On December 31, 1977 Sting held a New Year's Eve party. It had been a traumatic year and the last in which his face would remain truly his own.

CHAPTER TWO

OUTLANDOS D'AMOUR

"Sting, yeah that's right Sting. Sting as in bee. Sting as in stink without the K but with the G, my oh my we are having fun."

THE **S**ECOND Police single, released in the UK on April 9, 1978 went virtually unnoticed by the public. 'Roxanne' was written by Sting on October 20, 1977 after a visit to the red light district of Paris where The Police were playing at a club called The Nashville. The name Roxanne was taken from the lady whom Cyrano De Bergerac falls in love with in the play *Cyrano*, a personal favourite of Sting's. It is a stirring song about a man's love for a prostitute, a breed Sting described in *Record Mirror* as "an amazing phenomenon."

The song was something of a gamble, seen by Sting as little more than a throwaway track recorded during the 'Outlandos' sessions, which consisted mainly of putting their live set on tape. It was therefore with some trepidation that they played it to Miles Copeland, who never showed any particular interest in The Police anyway and only attended their rehearsals to pass on advice to his brother Stewart. He thought the material good but was knocked out when he heard 'Roxanne'. This was much to the band's surprise as the song was totally out of step with their other fast, harder-edged songs.

There are conflicting reports as to where 'Roxanne' actually surfaced. The Police were rehearsing in a cellar in Finchley, and with temperatures near zero things weren't going too well. Andy Summers remembers Sting playing parts of 'Roxanne' to him while in Paris. They messed around with it and were generally impressed. Miles walked in, thought most of the other tracks were rubbish but immediately recognised the potential of 'Roxanne'. By the very next day Miles had signed The Police to A&M, for whom Squeeze, another act managed by Miles, also recorded. A&M agreed to release 'Roxanne' but no advance would be paid; instead there would be a high royalty and the promise of release in America. This was a shrewd but calculated move by Copeland, and one which ensured that the three members of The Police would earn substantial wealth faster and in greater amounts than all of their punk contemporaries. Soon after this Miles became the band's manager. Sting was delighted. "I'd never had a record contract before, or even been near a record company. It was a milestone for me and I felt really good for the other two, especially Andy who had been in the business for a long time. I was an ex-school teacher and ex-semi-pro."

'Roxanne' was a milestone in other ways, as it was the first major hint of the influence reggae would play in Sting's songwriting. Reviews were glittering. "This must be the big breaker for The Police," hailed *Record Mirror*. "A beautiful entry, go out and buy it immediately." *Melody Maker* called it, "An amazing change of style. Could even be a minor hit if A&M do the groundwork." They didn't and it wasn't. 'Roxanne' fell flat, despite being Mick Jagger's favourite single at the time. It received no airplay and was kept off Radio One's playlist due to BBC hesitation over the song's subject matter. But The Police managed to earn enough from it to fly via Laker Airbus to America for a mini October/November tour. Miles, after years of managing profligate acts, was pioneering the budget tour but A&M were not keen on the idea as the group had no album to promote. "They told us not to come over," remarked Sting. "Because we'd be an embarrassment to them." With no financial support from their record company The Police went ahead regardless, though Miles did persuade A&M to make 'Roxanne' available in record stores and to radio stations across the continent.

They arrived in New York at 11pm on October 20, five hours late, giving them less than an hour to make the first gig at CBGB'S on Manhattan's lower East side. The 23-date tour that followed was as low budget as they come, travelling from city to city in a Ford custom panel van packed with essential equipment and one-man road crew Kim Turner. They played in any joint that would have them, from saloons to underground new wave discos in cities like New York, Toronto and Washington. They stayed in cheap hotels, sometimes two to a room. According to one report the three shared a double bed in one dive hotel. They restricted themselves to just 20 dollars a day expenses, spent mostly on fast food. On their return home Sting handed his wife $10 and said, "That's it, that's all we made."

Despite the hardships the tour was a resounding success, paving the way for similar US excursions by U2, Simple Minds and others. It certainly reaped greater rewards than had the band travelled as a support act with all the false hullabaloo of record company hype. However small the concerts, they made them their own, and as show followed show in quick succession they became a tight unit, cutting off dead flesh, defining what worked and what didn't, and ultimately becoming a polished and powerful act. The tour actually showed a profit, most unusual for a group with such limited experience, and 'Roxanne' began to chart in certain areas. This was largely due to a record store owner in Texas who persuaded his local radio station to play it. Listeners phoned in demanding more of the same and consequently word spread across the networks.

The Police were lucky too. At one concert which coincided with a big football game, they performed to only four people, Sting introduced them to one another and carried on as normal. A member of this audience just happened to be a DJ who began to play 'Roxanne'. In March and April the following year The Police returned for a second, more extensive tour. This time they had an album – 'Outlandos' – to promote and A&M were therefore enthusiastic about the band. Again The Police wisely refused financial aid, content to do it their way. While in New York publicity photos were taken inside a Harlem police station. A passing black woman asked if they were a pop group. "I hope they sound as good as The Bee Gees," she commented.

During this second US tour The Police were evidently seeking to break open the American market before the UK. 'Roxanne' became a top 40 hit and 'Outlandos' went top 30. At one show at The Bottom Line club in New York Robert Fripp, The B-52's and Daryl Hall were among the audience. Mick Jagger had also been asking for tickets. It was obvious to those who watched these live performances that the band's marriage of reggae and rock made them the most original act of the late seventies. Once damned for riding the punk bandwagon, applauded for introducing reggae rhythms to otherwise commercially orientated ears, yet condemned for trivialising a revered musical genre, they instead created a unique style and became one of the innovators of new wave.

The Police began recording 'Outlandos D'Amour' on January 13, 1978 at the Surrey Sound studios in Leatherhead, a 16-track studio run by Chris and

Nigel Gray. The band chose it for the natural sound quality of the rooms and the cheap rates, about £10 an hour. Recorded in fits and starts, it took until August to finish. The whole affair was self-financed. One of the more interesting stories relating to the recording concerned 'Roxanne'. Producer Nigel Gray: "On 'Roxanne' I laid the backing track first then the vocal. But because there are several long two-bar gaps, to get everybody to come back in on the beat directly after them was difficult. I finally did it by standing on the loudspeaker cabinet so they could all see me and conducting them." The album cost only £3,000 to make and was released on November 17, 1978. Raw is the best way to describe the record that launched The Police on their amazing journey to stardom. Side one is almost perfect. Three show-stoppers, 'Next To You' and 'So Lonely', delivered with punkish zeal and a hard rock punch, and 'Roxanne', cooling the proceedings down while foreshadowing the melodic rhythms that would come into their own on future albums. 'Hole In My Life' overstays its welcome somewhat leaving the excellent 'Peanuts' to bring the first side to a satisfying conclusion. The song was about Sting's one-time hero Rod Stewart. "I used to be a great fan of him but something happened to the guy. I hope I don't end up like that."

'Can't Stand Losing You' which opens side two was an obvious follow up single, while 'Truth Hits Everybody' and 'Born In The Fifties' are among the finest of Sting's early songs, displaying his talent for writing catchy pop compositions alongside such diverse offerings as 'Masoko Tanga', the album's closing track and a definite foretaste of 'Reggatta De Blanc'. Only Andy Summers' 'Be My Girl – Sally' lets the side down, with a narrative section out of place and context. Fans at the time certainly didn't agree; during their first headlining British tour crowds would chant the 'rubber doll' monologue word perfect.

On August 14 'Can't Stand Losing You' was released as the follow up to 'Roxanne', but in all manner of ways it suffered the same fate, failing to chart and running into censorship problems. This time the BBC were up in arms about the theme of threatened suicide and evidently refused to play it on the grounds that it contained the word 'kill'. "The BBC seem to be the arbiters of poetic metaphor at the present," Sting told the press. "The song wasn't meant to be taken seriously. I felt very strongly about 'Roxanne' though, and they wouldn't play that because it was about a prostitute. But write a silly song about 'fucking' that hasn't got the word 'fucking' in it and you've got a hit. It gets a bit depressing."

Reviews of the single were mixed. The harshest came from *NME*. "Great name for a feeble white reggae act, last observed proceeding in the direction of the waste bin." *Melody Maker* called it, "A neat piece of pop." Perhaps Neil Norman hit the nail on the head when he reviewed the band's Rock Garden gig in London. "They play with such energy and from a three-piece the power was remarkable. They are one of the few bands who have made me want to buy their singles on the grounds of their live performance. Someone lent me the latest one and I can't . . . I can't . . . I can't stop playing it." The picture sleeve also caused a minor uproar, with society's moralists failing to appreciate the wry humour in the stark image of Stewart with a noose around his neck standing on a block of ice slowly melting away next to a nearby heater. It remains a potent image and one of the best new wave sleeves ever.

'So Lonely' was released in November but like the others fared badly, despite a fair critical response. *Melody Maker* hailed it as a single worthy of consideration, while *Record Mirror* thought it, "A good album track which could be a minor hit." It finally became a silver disc top 10 smash when re-issued in 1980. A year earlier the previous singles were also re-released to coincide with The Police's new-found fame in America. 'Roxanne' reached the top 20 in April 1979 resulting in their first *Top Of The Pops* appearance on April 25.

Also the same month they embarked on a third US tour. Sting recalls the moment he knew 'Roxanne' was a hit was when he heard a workman whistling the tune outside his hotel room. "I thought, 'Blimey I've done it'. It's fantastic to write a song that anyone can whistle." 'Can't Stand Losing You' went even higher second time around, reaching number two in June. And on September 1 Sting achieved music journal fame when he appeared on the front cover of *NME*. It's interesting to note that neither Andy nor Stewart were in the picture: even this early on in their career Sting was treated as a solo personality. 'Outlandos D'Amour' eventually became the hit it deserved to be, reaching number six, helped by Annie Nightingale who regularly featured the band on her Sunday afternoon request show. By the end of 1979 the music paper polls showed evidence of Policemania. In the *Rolling Stone* critic's poll they were named best new artists and 'Outlandos' made a credible 46 in the top 100 album list. In the *Melody Maker* reader's poll The Police were second best band after Led Zeppelin, and second brightest hope, beaten by Gary Numan. 'Outlandos' was the fifth best album, 'Roxanne' fifth best single, 'Losing You' eighth and Sting was voted seventh best singer. Some start.

By the middle of 1979 The Police reached their highest pinnacle yet, headlining day one of the Reading Rock Festival. Also featured were The Cure and The Tourists, who featured future

Eurythmics Annie Lennox and Dave Stewart.
Before going on stage the trio were presented with
various awards at the A&M hospitality tent. Their
performance was triumphant, indeed by this time the
music press had come to expect little else. If anyone
was still in doubt that The Police had truly arrived,
their next single release 'Message In A Bottle'
became the most obvious number one of 1979.
The Police were on the fringes of super-stardom.

CHAPTER THREE

QUADROPHENIA

"I was in the movie just long enough to create a big impression, but not long enough to blow it."

IT WAS **H**ARDLY surprising that during the punk explosion a film would emerge which paralleled the frustration and search for individuality of this generation with that of their sixties cousins – the mods. As with the punks, music and fashion clearly dominated their cause, anti-establishment notions and the pretend politics of punks all vanished whenever their anthems hit the turntables. 'Anarchy In The UK' was the punk war cry, while The Who's 'My Generation' had earlier summed up what it was to be a mod. The basic look was simple: tight fitting single-breasted Italian-style suits and sharp gingham shirts on the inside, the fur lined parka, short hairstyle and Vespa scooter on the outside.

The mod scene sprang up amid the *Absolute Beginners* world of Soho's modern jazz clubs in the late fifties, swallowing up London and creating Carnaby Street in its wake. It ended in headline notoriety on the beaches of resorts like Brighton and Southend, where meaningless clashes between mods and their arch enemies the rockers attracted media hysteria and strong-arm police tactics. *Quadrophenia* was set in 1964, the year of the beach battles. Phil Daniels portrays dedicated mod Jimmy, the film's main character, a pill-popping society freak whose otherwise mundane existence comes to life only when he slips on his mod gear. His friends are mods and the whole film leads up to a notorious Brighton weekend onslaught which is the highlight of the film. It's here that Sting makes his feature film début, riding into town with a scooter entourage like a modern-day cowboy. He is seen again at the local ballroom attracting female attention with his cool dancing and it is on the dance floor that he utters his first celluloid line. "Fuck off," he shouts when pushed by a fellow dancer. An auspicious start indeed.

In his movie début Sting plays Ace Face. In mod jargon a 'face' was a leading figure in the movement whose style was admired by others, indeed The Who's first single was 'I'm The Face'. It was Frances who persuaded him to audition for the role. Before he had only appeared in a handful of TV commercials, again on his wife's advice, which included a Brutus Jeans ad and a Triumph bra commercial. "I had to grope Joanna Lumley's tits," he recalled. For a Wrigley chewing gum ad for American television he won parts for the other Police members to play punk rockers. "Stewart already had blond hair, Andy and I had to dye ours. It's stayed that way ever since." Despite looking fairly extraordinary . . . "I had this shock of blond hair with green bits on the side . . .", he never failed to win the television ads he auditioned for but was still hesitant about the *Quadrophenia* audition.

At a studio in Wardour Street he met Franc Roddam, the director, and sat discussing Newcastle and a book they had both read. After an hour Roddam said, "I've got to stop now, turn round." Sting obliged. "OK do you want the job?" asked Roddam. "It was as simple as that. All I had to do was look the part. My role was more of a fantasy in an otherwise realistic film. That look on Ace's face when Jimmy attempts to upstage him at a dance, that was my natural expression. I don't like being upstaged."

In 1981 Sting spoke to *NME* about his role. "That wasn't me in *Quadrophenia* at all. I was nothing to do with mods. When the whole mod revival happened we exploited it and for a brief while I became its figure-head. People ask me now what I think of mods, well I don't like them, I'd rather have a motorbike. But it was well used, I'd wear a parka at the odd gig." In an interview for *Record Mirror* he elaborated: "I don't think I could have done *Quadrophenia* if it had been a stage show. I couldn't sustain a character for so long. Acting in front of a camera is easy in that respect, you only have to keep it up for a few seconds."

Quadrophenia was unveiled at the Cannes Film Festival and was well received. Launched in Britain as the UK equivalent of Walter Hill's *The Warriors*, it was backed up with a massive publicity campaign. The album was released again, a tie-in book was published and trailers drenched the TV networks. The film got an added push when The Who played Wembley Stadium only days after the movie's opening, a gig attended by Sting. Much the same tactic was employed in Los Angeles.

Quadrophenia opened with a bang on August 14, 1979 at London's Plaza Cinema with a gala première. Sting, The Who and cast members attended, but the headlines were seized by a legion of mods who turned out for the event, filling Lower Regent Street with their scooters. The film grossed £36,472 in seven West End days. In many houses it broke records and continued a healthy financial existence throughout the country. By the end of the year it was eighth in the top 10 list of successful pictures of 1979.

The story on the other side of the Atlantic, the main market, was less joyous. Along with other Rank offerings of the period like *Scum* and *Rude Boy*, all realistic British youth films, *Quadrophenia* failed to attract a major distributor, even though many believed it would succeed where other UK rock films like *Stardust* had failed. In America *Quadrophenia* remains sadly undiscovered by mainstream audiences, reduced to midnight movie theatres or college campus screens, and lying very much in the cult cupboard.

British critics universally acclaimed the picture. *The Daily Telegraph* called it, "Disturbingly accurate and violent," while *The Guardian* was also impressed . . . "The tone of the film is just right, managing the transition from social comedy to something like tragedy with scarcely a false move." *NME* called it, "The best British film of 1979 and probably the finest British rock film ever." Andy Summers, once a rocker himself, thought the movie more than authentic. But the most positive review of Sting came from *Films In Review*: "The star of the Brighton siege is Sting, who for my money delivers the kind of flash and intensity that hasn't been seen since James Dean. If for no other reason see *Quadrophenia* for this guy." Sting's cameo appearance in *Quadrophenia* was perfectly timed. With 'Reggatta De Blanc' released two months after the film's UK opening, it proved advantageous in increasing its sales and pushing Sting further into the limelight. But it also worked the other way; the success of The Police made *Quadrophenia* more appealing and accessible to the growing number of Police followers around the world, being released in Australia for example, after the group had toured there.

Quadrophenia is a perfectly realised film and was an ideal début vehicle for Sting. "That film really chose me," he explains. "At that stage in my career I took what was offered, I wasn't known and the band hadn't really made it yet. They used me as a face. I think it was a good film all round and that part was very useful."

It's interesting to note that towards the end of 1979 Sting was being referred to as an ex-model, an actor, a singer and a bass player. Even at the beginning of his career with The Police he was seen as a multi-talented performer. In one interview, asked if things had changed for him since *Quadrophenia*, he replied, "Of course, I'm rich and famous now."

CHAPTER FOUR

REGGATTA DE BLANC

"We played a gig in West Virginia to five people the day we were number one in England."

THE **N**UMBER one in question was 'Message In A Bottle', released on September 7, 1979, and one of the group's most popular singles. It became the definitive song of the year, a perfect musical bridge between decades. It couldn't have come at a better time either, as if the group's rise, and Sting's in particular, had been preordained, topping the charts around the time of *Quadrophenia*'s general release. Sting became a pin-up idol, his face staring out from magazine covers as diverse as *NME* and *Woman's Own*.

The two other Policemen had clear views on the single. Andy called it the best track he'd ever played on and, at that time, ideal Police music. Stewart commented. "All the time I spend doodling in the studio Sting just stands there looking out of a window. But at the end of it he'll come up with something like 'Message In A Bottle'."

"I think the lyrics are subtle and well crafted enough to hit people on a different level from just something you sing along with," Sting said of the song. "It's quite a cleverly put together metaphor, it develops and has an artistic shape to it. I'm very proud of that song."

Reviews were on the whole pleasing, *NME* being the most positive. "Police singles are the rock counterpart to Chic, the most distinctive charismatic sound around." By the end of the year *NME* chose 'Message' as their sixth best single of 1979. Surprisingly other papers responded less enthusiastically. "As mild as paint stripper and the neighbours will complain," said *Melody Maker*, while *Record Mirror* called it, "Smoother than usual, obviously softened up for the American market." But curiously the single and the album both met with a lukewarm response in the States, especially considering the earlier hysteria over the group, and they left for a fourth US tour at the end of September to whip up dangerously flagging Yankee interest.

For their second album 'Reggatta De Blanc' (a joke spelling of White Reggae), the group returned to Nigel Gray's Surrey Sound Studio, by this time upgraded to 24 tracks. Even though A&M had pressured them to record in a fully professional studio the trio retained their faith in Nigel and began recording there on February 13, 1979. For 'Reggatta' The Police actually rehearsed very little, unlike the 'Outlandos' sessions which physically and mentally wrecked the band. Thanks to the rigorous American tours they were now so musically in tune with one another that the arrangements for the songs were gathered and completed without much struggle.

"We just went in and did the job," said Sting. "We're that sort of group." However he did admit to having little faith in the project. "I was worried sick basically. I kept asking Nigel whether he really thought we had an album. I couldn't hear it or feel it. It all seemed dreadful to me. I had no confidence in it." But belief in his and the band's talents still reigned. "Reggatta will show a few changes," he claimed. "It's surprising how flexible the three-piece format is, and Andy's influence is a bit more extensive. I'm starting to find a wider range in my voice too."

'Reggatta De Blanc' gave the public a new Police sound. The shackles of punk were gone and the reggae echoes of 'Roxanne' dominated the tracks, giving the album a noticeably more experimental feel. But some critics considered it a disappointment after the power of its predecessor. 'Cops Cop Out' read the caption on *Record Mirror*'s review, "Next time they're going to have to do better." Others were less harsh: "The important development here is that they know the potential of this LP," said *NME*. "While nobody really understood what they had with the début. An investment." *Melody Maker* justly raved about it: "The first four tracks should be enough to convince even cloth-eared sceptics that The Police are about to be the biggest trio since Cream." When released in the first week of October 1979 the public ate it up making 'Reggatta De Blanc' the band's first number one album, but certainly not their last.

By this time Sting had become the most seen and talked about new celebrity of the late seventies. With a hit album and single and a major movie, *Quadrophenia* to his credit it was an understatement when *Record Mirror* said, "If there is to be a face of '79 it has to be Sting's." When he appeared on *Juke Box Jury* on August 11 the BBC were inundated with calls from female viewers. During this period Sting lived in a modest two bedroom basement flat in Bayswater, his name clearly emblazoned on the doorbell. He could often be seen sitting in a movie director's chair in his living room, the red canvas stretched over the wooden frame sporting in bold white letters the name of its proud owner. Sometimes when he rested in the basement yard passing girls would look down, shout gleefully and ask for autographs. "I don't mind being asked," he said. "But some girls come back day after day and then I have to be firm. I put on my school teacher voice and that frightens them away."

With The Police now leading the way for new groups into the eighties, the stigma of their neo-punk heritage was all but lost in the swell of new-found fame on their own terms. "Punk's not where I'm at," declared Sting on the eve of the new decade. "To be a rock 'n' roll star? Well maybe I'm ready to take that on." Sting believed The Police to be closer to Abba than they were to The Clash. "I don't see any disgrace in that." There is much truth in this statement: along with Abba and a few others, The Police became one of the great quintessential singles bands. Sting often quipped that The Police's best album would be a compilation record of their hits.

The video for 'Message In A Bottle' was a more satisfactory work than any of the promos made for the 'Outlandos' singles, which consisted mainly of blank concert footage. Performing within the confines of a dressing room, the breezy and spontaneous zest that would permeate most of their future video work is in evidence here for the first time, and it is clear that the trio are enjoying themselves and not worried about relaying any message to the viewer.

The follow-up single, 'Walking On The Moon', released in November due to overwhelming demand, also reached number one. Sting apparently wrote the song in a hotel room in Munich. He had been drinking in some disco and on his return started singing the song's riff while 'walking around the room', the song's original title. This isn't generally the method Sting uses to write his songs though. "I work backwards and build a song around a hook rather than start from A and work to Z," he disclosed. "They're not straight reggae songs. What I do is weld elements of reggae into a rock setting."

The video for 'Walking On The Moon' saw the group playing and messing around at the Cape

Andy Phillips

Below:
With Chelsea's Gene
October at The
Greyhound, Fulham
September 1981.
(Andy Phillips)

Top:
With Police manager Miles Copeland.
(Andy Phillips)

Police 1981. *(LFI.)*

Attending the premiere of Pink Floyd's 'The Wall' film, February 1982. *(Pictorial Press)*

Below:
With former wife Francis Tomelty. *(Pictorial Press)*

With Trudie Styler and
daughter Brigitte
Michaele, December
1984. *(Pictorial Press)*

With Trudie Styler at the
London premiere of the
film '1984', October
1984. *(Pictorial Press)*

Canaveral space centre, with Stewart drumming on the fuselage of a billion-dollar rocket. This fixation of Copeland's for beating on any object available reached an amusing peak in their next video, 'So Lonely', re-issued in February 1980 and reaching number six. Set in Japan the group ride the Tokyo subway looking very CIA and singing into walkie-talkie units. Stewart drums on everything from police jeeps to passing buses and signposts. But the highlight comes when he attempts to play on large coffee jars outside a market shop; the irate owner runs out and sends him scurrying away. Thus Copeland became firmly established as the clown of the group.

During the success of 'Reggatta' The Police maintained a steady flow of stage appearances, notably an October gig before 900 inmates at an all-male prison on Terminal Island, San Pedro, California – a result of the group donating equipment to the prison's music programme as part of Miles Copeland's policy of helping deserving projects. "It was about that time we began to think of some of our social responsibilities," he said.

In Britain around Christmas The Police pulled off a remarkable publicity coup by playing both the Hammersmith venues, Palais and Odeon, on the same night, December 18. Over 40 police officers were on duty to keep order as thousands of fans lined the streets to watch the group escorted in a half-truck army personnel carrier from one venue to the other. Many likened the scenes to the hysteria of mid-sixties Beatlemania. It was exactly what Miles wanted, the group to end the decade in a blaze of headline glory. They also added an extra show on the Christmas tour at the Lewisham Odeon on December 22. It went under the handle, 'Reggatta De Cats' and the price of a ticket was a toy, all of which were given to Dr Barnado's homes.

'Reggatta De Blanc' practically swept the polls by the year's end. It was the best LP in the *Record Mirror* readers' poll and numerous others. It picked up a staggering five Grammy nominations including best album and best song for 'Message In A Bottle'. Back home though *NME* ranked the album a poor 24, but Paul Morley in his 1979 retrospective described The Police as 'probably' the band of the year. On a lighter note Paula Yates erroneously bestowed upon Sting 'The Natural Blonde Award'.

At the end of the year Sting told *Melody Maker* The Police would last for three albums, "I think there are very few groups worth any more, and being an older group we're aware of the suicidal nature of what we do. I've no illusions about being a star tomorrow." Indeed the hardest stage was yet to come, the perilous third album. But before that the group embarked on what was then the most extensive world tour ever undertaken by a rock band: almost four months of concerts in 15 countries taking in almost 37 cities. The Police were now entering the history book league.

CHAPTER FIVE

RADIO ON

*"I just sit in a caravan singing 'Three Steps
To Heaven', it's not exactly Ben Hur."*

RIDING **H**IGH on complimentary reviews for
Quadrophenia, Sting's second feature film *Radio
On* could hardly have come at a better time, barely
four months after The Who movie and two months
on from the release of 'Reggatta'. It was another
cameo appearance, this time as a garage hand
obsessed with Eddie Cochran. But any effect the
film could have had in elevating Sting's career to
yet dizzier heights was lost due to the picture's
minority interest, appealing to art house audiences
only. Currently unavailable on video, to date never
shown on television, it remains something of a
black and white curiosity object.

As an independent movie and hardly mainstream
material, first-time film maker Chris Petit, a
former cinema writer with *Time Out*, found the
road to securing a workable budget for his project
an arduous one. Back in January 1977 while
writing the first draft of *Radio On* Petit
interviewed Wim Wenders, who was in London to
publicise *The American Friend*, one of Sting's
favourite films. Petit secured Wenders' interest and
was told to keep in touch.

Meanwhile several attempts to win backing in
Britain had failed. Producers were hesitant and
The National Film Finance Corporation turned it
down outright for being too pretentious. At the
close of 1977 Petit met Wenders again and together
they struck up a partnership. Wenders promised
that if half the money could be found from British
sources he would match the rest from Germany.

Eventually 30 per cent of the budget came from Wenders' own 'Road Movie' company, the rest from UK backers, The Production Board and The NFFC, who had become interested again when Petit approached them with a name actor who later had to pull out.

Sting sings for the cinema camera for the first time in *Radio On* when he performs Eddie Cochran's 'Three Steps To Heaven', as a tribute to the singer who died in 1960 on his way to Heathrow Airport from the Bristol Hippodrome.

His agents Plant And Froggit sent him along for the part and he won it with little difficulty. Afterwards he commented: "It was nice to have been in *Radio On* because it was very obscure. It was perfect and I enjoyed being in it, I got about £20. I loved Chris's way of directing where I could just be myself."

Sting made another film around this time, the infamous *Great Rock 'n' Roll Swindle*. His part had him molesting Sex Pistols' drummer Paul Cook in the back of a Chevrolet, but the scenes were left on the cutting room floor. "Thank God it's been cut out," said a relieved Sting. "I hated the part and the director was a real jerk, but I needed the money really badly."

Radio On was premièred at the Edinburgh Film Festival and went on selected release in November 1979, though it only played in art houses like London's Screen On The Hill.

Overall it met with positive reviews . *The Times* called it, "A film of personality, skill and flair." *The Guardian* went a stage further. "It is a reverberating original début which, like it or lump it, is a genuine breakthrough." On the negative side *The Motion Picture Guide* commented: "While the premise is interesting and needs to be explored in British films, the pace remains slow. The film is an indictment on the state of England today." The worst critic was *Record Mirror* who thought the film had all the appeal of onion-flavoured toothpaste. Despite this carefully considered opinion *Radio On* went on to win the special jury prize for the most striking and original first feature at the Taormina Film Festival in Sicily. *Radio On* is very much a first film. As Jean-Luc Godard said in a Christmas interview for *Cahiers Du Cinema* in 1962, "Our first films were all 'films de cinephile', the work of film enthusiasts." Petit's *Radio On* shares with other first films, Wenders' *Summer In The City* (1970) and Godard's *Breathless* (1959), the idea of a film maker addressing his contemporary landscape in an entirely cinematic fashion, in Petit's case through the use of car window travelling shots of passing streets, people and buildings. This was no more apparent than in the poster design for *Radio On* which features the view from a car's front window of a metropolis horizon.

CHAPTER SIX

ZENYATTA MONDATTA

"I've always said that I like money. I'm not happier because I'm rich but it certainly dulls the pain."

ON **M**ARCH 25, 1980 The Police became the first Western rock band to perform in India, a historic event made the more unusual by the absence of any major promoter. Instead the concerts were partly organised by The Time And Talents Club, a group of old women who usually presided over jumble sales and classical music recitals. Both nights at Bombay's Homi Bha Bha were sold out, and though the city's upper class denizens were the ticket holding majority, a series of mini-riots resulted in the lower classes gaining access to give the audience a much needed fervour. Sting helped by ordering the crowd to dance or else. The star later remarked that the Bombay gigs were the best he had yet witnessed, confirming his belief in music as a universal phenomenon effective anywhere. These concerts were charity events and raised over £10,000.

This was all part of The Police's grand world tour. They had already played Japan and Hong Kong but while in New Zealand Sting suffered a throat infection after only the first night, resulting in that leg of the tour being cancelled. After Australia and Bombay they went on to Cairo and observed the base sights for which the Third World is famous, starving children and beggars, images horribly common in such societies. "It's obviously a good thing for The Police to play the Third World," Miles Copeland commented at the time. "Besides the international exposure, it gets to the youth of these countries, people who will one day be running them."

In Cairo the atmosphere was red hot. The recently ousted Shah of Iran had been given sanctuary by Anwar Sadat close to the Holiday Inn where The Police were staying, and the area was thick with armed troops. Add to that the group's own mini-brigade of hired bodyguards who followed the trio everywhere, and the result was a potentially explosive situation. The concert almost didn't happen because of a poor PA and lighting system, but all was saved by a film crew travelling with the band recording events, and a team from *The Old Grey Whistle Test* who both lent them their lights. This unnecessary pressure resulted in Sting losing patience, quite rightly, with a fat bouncer who was molesting sections of the audience. The humiliated man turned out to be the chief of police, and at the concert's end he was backstage with an escort demanding an apology. Sting refused to comply, leaving Miles with the unenviable task of charming the group's exit visas from the irate official.

Things improved only marginally in Greece and Italy. In Athens, where The Police were the first rock band to perform since The Rolling Stones in 1969, genuine hysteria greeted them, and their passage to the gig was blocked for an hour by thousands of fans. In Italy everything got out of control. Originally scheduled to appear in Rome, The Police had been denied that privilege due to the capital's riot record.

Ironically at the lesser known Reggio Emilia there were ugly scenes and street battles between fans and the more prepared riot police, who used tear gas which managed to get backstage. It was nothing less than a war zone. "But remember," Miles told Sting just as he was about to go on-stage. "All this is great for the movie." To which the world-weary star replied. "I'll remember that when they rush the stage and start tearing us to pieces, it'll be very reassuring." On October 10, 1980 the BBC showed *Police In The East*, the documentary of their world tour. Sting's death was not included.

After more European concerts the momentous tour ended prematurely on April 19. The cause was again Sting's voice which gave out midway through a German gig in Hanover. Kim Turner pulled the plug on Sting's instruction halfway through 'Roxanne', and a technical fault took the blame as The Police sped away into the night.

Nine days later the band officially closed their world tour with two sentimental concerts in Sting's home town of Newcastle. In April The Police formed their own charity organisation 'The Outlandos Trust', its aim to finance mainly music-orientated youth projects. Because the band were now huge earners, they were liable to vicious tax demands which forced them to flee abroad, though in their case only temporarily. In June Sting moved to Ireland, buying a cottage on the west coast, he also bought a London house in Hampstead. The press were surprisingly lenient over the tax dodge, but still brought up the subject of money in all interviews. When Sting was asked where all his money was he replied, "It's all on paper but I haven't really got it. Next year I'll be rich and that's when the rot could set in. I'm aware that money corrupts." In the same year he also observed, "It's all very well having bank notes up to here, but when the bomb drops it's worth fuck all."

Tax reasons prevented the third Police album from being recorded in Britain. Instead the Wisseloord studio in Holland was chosen with Nigel Gray again producing. Sting brought to the sessions a myriad of basses and one double bass in order to achieve a richer sound. The average working day saw the band toiling from midday to midnight, a strict régime imposed on them by A&M who had given them just one month from July 7 to complete the sessions. Sting was under a great obligation as The Police had now become a mini-business with dozens of people relying on the forthcoming record. "Men and women with kids to feed now depend on the success of the next Police single to pay the rent," he said. "That's a fact, we support an entire industry." In another interview he jokingly replied to accusations that the band had become a small business. "We're more like a chain of shops. The Police are the Marks and Spencer of rock 'n' roll."

These rigid conditions weren't ideal and the recording of 'Zenyatta Mondatta' suffered as a result.'Nigel Gray found it difficult working in another studio, and thought the album would have been better recorded in surroundings more familiar to the group. They also had to interrupt proceedings by honouring a commitment to play several charity concerts.

On July 26 they headlined the first ever rock show at the Milton Keynes bowl. It was a wet, muddy affair, further marred by a break-in at the trio's caravan and the theft of Sting's stage clothes. The following day The Police played Leixlip castle in Dublin supported by, among others, U2. However, the crowd behaved shamefully and on entering the arena Sting was almost hit by a bottle. Later Stewart, who wasn't so lucky, took a direct hit.

Released on October 3, 1980, 'Zenyatta Mondatta' was greeted with derision by the critics. *NME* reviewed it under the banner, 'The Policeman's Balls Up' and commented that it sounded, "Like something a shyster would dredge up from the vaults, out-takes and such to milk the nostalgic market should The Police meet their maker in an aircraft crash." *Melody Maker* called it a, "grade D failure". *Sounds* however found reason to bestow praise, giving it four stars, and agreeing with the public who made it number one almost immediately. Miles Copeland jubilantly confided that the album had sold more in its first three weeks of release than the rest of the top 10 put together. It also put the band back on top in America after the disappointing response to 'Reggatta'. By Christmas 1980 both the album and its second single release 'De Do Do Do' were among the 20 best selling records in the USA. But it remains their least satisfactory album.

"While I was writing it I was getting letters from the record company saying retailers were waiting for it which didn't help," admitted Sting. "I'm not offering excuses for 'Zenyatta'. I think it's a reasonable pop album and I'll defend certain songs. It had some good moments. It had some really terrible moments too."

One of the finest tracks was the first single, 'Don't Stand So Close To Me'. Released on September 19 it became the band's third consecutive number one, making The Police one of the few bands ever to achieve this feat. Its success, alleged sales of half a million copies in its first week in Britain alone, saw The Police at the peak of their popularity, and the accompanying video was their most perfectly realised to date. Set in a classroom, Sting plays a mock teacher with Victorian black gown (an outfit he wore when performing the number on stage), angel's wings and symbolic carpet beater. "We shot it at a real school," he explained. "It didn't tell a story, we just clowned around with me wielding a cane." The song, which deals with a schoolgirl's crush on a teacher, was interpreted by some as an ironic reference to Sting's academic past. But the main inspiration was from the novel *Lolita* by Vladimir Nabakov. "I did teach in a secondary school for a time," he said. "But although I did think about it I wasn't guilty of deflowering any virgins."

Other notable tracks included 'When The World Is Running Down', 'Canary In A Coalmine' and 'De Do Do Do, De Da Da Da', a top 10 hit in December and later recorded in Japanese and Spanish. But Sting was angry that the song was misunderstood. "The lyrics are about banality and the abuse of words," he told NME. "Almost everyone who reviewed it said 'Oh this is baby talk'. They were just listening to the chorus alone. It's quite a serious song, but because it's by The Police it was written off as being garbage."

The most worthy song was 'Driven To Tears', recorded independently on March 16 in Melbourne and used so poignantly five years later at Live Aid. "It was just a personal reaction to watching the Third World die on TV every night. Reading a colour supplement and seeing pictures of a kid well on the way to a nasty death." This was the first time that the star had revealed his feelings on a particular world issue through a song, and can therefore be seen as a definite milestone in his songwriting career, paving the way for 'Invisible Sun' and much of his solo work.

The last months of 1980 were taken up by yet another long hard tour. In October The Sun ran a piece on just how fit Sting was. He ran three miles each day, did 30 sit ups, 50 push ups and an hour of muscle exercises and arm wrestling with a bodyguard newly employed after he was mobbed by fans in Dublin. The tour took in the entire American continent from Vancouver to Buenos Aires. The punishing schedule finally took its toll in Miami where the singer's voice became infected again and the South American gigs were cut short. The Police finished 1980, their most productive year yet, with open air British dates at Tooting Bec

Common and Stafford. However, although the Stafford concert succeeded, the Tooting shows on December 21 and 22 failed miserably. They were held in a huge 5,000 capacity super-tent, but the press complained about the overcrowding. People fainted, some were even injured. "Since when," quipped Sting, "has rock 'n' roll been a comfortable experience?"

CHAPTER SEVEN

GHOST IN THE MACHINE

"If one person reads the book because our album has the same title, then I think it's a good excuse to have called it that."

AFTER THE commercialism of 'Zenyatta', the fourth Police album was more positive, deeper and less superficial than its half-baked predecessor. 'Ghost In The Machine' was certainly a radical departure from their previous work, more lyrically esoteric, discussing among other topics the philosophical theories explored in Arthur Koestler's book of the same name, which Sting had read in 1976. The book attacks behaviourist psychology, the programming of thinking minds to behave in a conformist manner, and much of its influence is reflected in songs on the album.

The two most obvious are 'Demolition Man', about the beast within us and its destructive nature, a song originally written for 'Zenyatta' and later covered by Grace Jones, and 'Re-Humanise Yourself', which parallels Koestler's idea that society is gradually dehumanising itself. The remaining songs, many of which contain threads of the book's theme, tackle other moral issues while others return to the reggae-based dance tempo of 'Reggatta', notably 'One World (Not Three)'. 'Spirits In The Material World', the album's opener, illustrates Sting's disillusion with the political system's ability to solve global problems. "My songs are apolitical," he said. "I hate politics, I hate politicians, I hate the mess they've made of the world." 'Every Little Thing She Does Is Magic', is a simple love song written by Sting five years before, along with 'Invisible Sun', the LP's showcase track.

'Hungry For You' continues the romantic theme. "It's in French," said Sting. "Because it's filthy and French is the language of love." 'Too Much Information' is a denouncement of mass communication, of drowning in too much news, and 'One World (Not Three)' a plea for a unified planet. Both this track and 'Demolition Man' were apparently recorded in one take. 'Omega Man' and 'Darkness' are Summers and Copeland tracks respectively with Sting's 'Secret Journey', based on the book *Meetings With Remarkable Men*, sandwiched in between.

After the foul weather of Holland (Sting recalled that it rained there for four straight weeks), The Police decided to record 'Ghost' in sunnier climes, George Martin's studio in Montserrat in the Caribbean. Since Nigel Gray was absent, noted producer Hugh Padgham took over the production reins during six weeks of recording which began on June 15, 1981. The album was mixed in Montreal in late August and the band reportedly had 15 tracks to choose from. Also around this time tapes were mixed for a proposed live double album, recorded around the world since 1979. Sadly it never materialised.

Along with new ideas, new sounds emerged on the album, with Sting performing saxophone on some songs. He had played the instrument in his teens, but had to re-learn his technique for the 'Ghost' sessions. He also experimented with arranging his own brass sections, later actualised in the form of 'Chops', a three-piece horn section who joined the band on tour. Sting's voice was also different. "It has a greater range now," Andy Summers noted. "In the old days I thought he used to sound like Yes's Jon Anderson."

The most overt changes were visual. Though the album's title was in English for the first time it was still unorthodox, with the group's faces absent from the cover. Instead they were presented as computerised images; squeeze your eyes tightly and you get the effect. This was a conscious move away from a high public profile and the image of three nutty blonds just having a good time.

The album's contents offered further evidence of this progression, "This album is an important step," Sting told *Melody Maker*. "Everyone was expecting a sequel to the last three which didn't happen. I don't need another number one, it was more important to produce something of integrity." Perhaps Sting had now grown tired of the fame game, or more likely just come to terms with it. "But I still get paranoid. Some mornings I wake up in a cold sweat and think, 'Fuck I'm famous', I'll walk out into the street and people are going to know who I am."

A change in the group's style was apparent in the first single from 'Ghost', 'Invisible Sun', a song about the situation in Northern Ireland and its effect on the inhabitants. The video, a series of stark black and white images of soldiers and the streets of Belfast, was banned by the BBC and the otherwise credible *Tiswas*. Sting was not slow in reacting to the ban. "Of course the ultimate irony is that you'll get Legs And Co fucking dancing to it in sombreros and sun tan oil thinking it's about the sun. I don't give a shit." Later in more serious mood he added, "I can see why the BBC turned it down. But I disagree, I think it should be shown for exactly those reasons."

Sting pointed out that the overall message of 'Invisible Sun' wasn't political, just a presentation of fact. Indeed Frances Tomelty, herself from Belfast, was present at the editing stage of the promo, balancing the Protestant and Catholic viewpoint and ensuring the end product was non-sectarian.

'Every Little Thing She Does Is Magic', the group's next single, was a return to their earlier fun-style videos and more commercial pop sound, and it became a number one smash, unlike 'Invisible Sun' which only reached number two. The 'Every Little Thing' promo at times resembled 'Message In A Bottle' in that it had the trio performing within a closed space, this time a studio control room. Their antics here, chiefly Andy's walk across the recording console, represented the last of The Police's fun videos.

'Ghost In The Machine' was unveiled to a potentially hostile music press on October 2, 1981, but received favourable reviews. The release coincided with Sting's 30th birthday. "It's an interesting time to reassess and plan ahead and think of yourself at the end of the next decade," he said. "I also looked back on the last 10 years, an abortive university career, a career as a teacher, and now I'm a 30-year-old millionaire, hah."

Frances Tomelty related how much Sting had altered over those years. "The interesting thing is how much Sting has changed. He thinks he hasn't but he has, enormously. You can't take someone who was a school teacher from Newcastle, then suddenly five years later after all he's been through expect him to be the same person. I remember the first time he flew. He was terrified, he was 26 and had never been in a plane before. He really was a very inexperienced boy."

'Spirits In The Material World', the final single off the album, failed to reach the heights of the previous two, only reaching number 12, but still left The Police as popular as ever by the year's end. It was a year that had started with yet another world tour, taking in America, Japan, Australia and New Zealand. The most prestigious gig was at New York's Madison Square Garden on January 10. During 'De Do Do Do', a vodka bottle was thrown at the stage puncturing the bass drum. Sting improvised and got the crowd singing 'The Yellow Rose Of Texas', while repairs went ahead behind him. "I hadn't ad-libbed for a long time," he said. "In the early days things always went wrong. Today we normally run like clockwork. But I think ultimately that incident helped us to show our human side."

Photographer Joe Stevens was impressed with Sting that night. "I've seen Springsteen up close," he said. "And to get to the people at the back he fakes quite a bit. But Sting didn't seem at all contrived." The best quote about the incident must be Sting's own: "A real super group would have left. We three arseholes just stood there."

The Police played two other noteworthy gigs in America during January. The first was a secret mini-gig at The Ritz in New York, where reports disclosed that people could feel the balcony shaking, while the second was a bizarre concert at the small LA Variety Arts Theatre where no one was admitted without blond wigs. The band later walked on-stage wearing false black hair.

In September Sting took part in two diverse events. He performed 'Roxanne' and 'Message In A Bottle' at *The Secret Policeman's Other Ball*, held at London's Theatre Royal for Amnesty International, alongside stars like Billy Connolly, Phil Collins and Eric Clapton. He also guested at a gig by the group Chelsea in The Greyhound pub, Fulham and was reported as saying that the experience had been as nerve-racking as Wembley. In December The Police played that very arena, and utilised a massive back projection screen to present the banned 'Invisible Sun' video while the song was performed.

The first half of 1982 saw the group on tour again, with dates in Europe and an extensive visit to North and South America. For Sting the hard rigour of touring proved the calm before the storm for by the year's end he would be involved in a bitter court case and his seven-year marriage to Frances Tomelty would hit the rocks.

CHAPTER EIGHT

BRIMSTONE AND TREACLE

*"Which of the seven deadly sins is my speciality.
Pride, greed, I have them all, I'm the jack of
all sins."*

AFTER **H**IS début in *Quadrophenia* and the sudden rise
to prominence of The Police, Sting was inundated
with movie offers in the early eighties. The most
prestigious was the role of a villain in the James
Bond movie *For Your Eyes Only*. He appeared to
be interested in the idea and exploited the media
attention but ultimately declined. "I went to see it
in New York," he said. "But it was so boring I
walked out. It's sad because the Bond films as a
genre have been very entertaining, I've grown up
with them. I loved *Goldfinger* and all that. To see
the arse end of the series was very sad."
He was also asked to portray Mordred in John
Boorman's *Knights Of The Round Table*, which
later became *Excalibur*, and the marathon runner
John Tarrant in the proposed film *Ghost Runner*.
He also turned down a role in *The Jazz Singer* and
the part of a rock star in a Francis Ford Coppola
production. "The offer was attractive," he
admitted. "But on reading the script it was the
stereotype pop star with his stereotype problems.
I decided that what I'd get out of working in that
movie wouldn't be worth the price of failing in it."
He was also offered the part of another rock star,
one who is attacked and goes on to seek vengeance,
in a movie to be called *While My Guitar Gently
Weeps*, and turned down a role in the Royal
Shakespeare Company's production of
The Tempest.

After considering all of these proposals Sting
wisely chose *Brimstone And Treacle*, a low budget
British feature based on a disturbing television play
by Dennis Potter, who also adapted it for the
screen. The central character, a young man called
Martin Taylor, worms his way into the household
of a miserable middle aged couple whose daughter,
the victim of a road accident, lies in a permanently
catatonic state in their front living room.
Originally written for the small screen in 1976, it
was considered by Alastair Milne, then BBC
director of programming, unsuitable for
transmission because of its subject matter and a
scene in which Martin rapes the helpless daughter.
Banned three days before broadcasting, Milne's
decision caused a flood of controversy; many
feared it would lead to stricter media censorship,
while others (after viewing it at the Edinburgh TV
Festival) sent telegrams of protest. But Milne stuck
to his original argument, laid out in a letter to
Potter quoted in *The New Statesman* on April 23,
that the rape scene would cause such outrage that
the author's 'point of serious importance' would be
lost in the controversy. It remained publicly
unseen for many years, though there were two
theatre productions in 1977 and 1979.
The decision to turn *Brimstone And Treacle* into
a film certainly made box office sense, as did the
cinema version of Roy Minton's *Scum*, another
banned BBC play made in 1980 with
Quadrophenia's Phil Daniels. *Brimstone* finally
appeared in the summer of 1982 when the
controversy over its initial banning had long been
forgotten. What made the most box office sense
was the casting of Sting in the lead role.
"It's definitely a good movie for me. A real coup,
a real acting part," he enthused. Other more
established actors had already been approached
including David Bowie, who proved unavailable,

and Michael Palin. When Sting met director Richard Loncraine in 1981 in New York, he was on a short list along with Malcolm McDowell, whom he curiously resembles in the finished film. At four o'clock in the morning they walked from one fast food joint to another discussing the project. "I think his powers of judgement were a little impaired at the time," joked Sting. "So I managed to convince him that I should be Taylor. We never looked back."

He was an obvious choice considering the character's ambivalence, a trait which attracted him because of his fascination with the theme of good and bad existing within the same person. "He's both good and evil," Sting revealed. "Genuinely religious but also full of sexual frustration. He's much more interesting than other cinematic characters. He is a kind of nice boy, well mannered, but also quite nasty, one minute you're laughing, the next you're squirming. That's why I wanted to make the film."

Sting identified with Martin's physical appearance. "He's not polished, he's got rough edges, hasn't shaved, his eyes are baggy. He's closer to the real me, nearer to the truth than the glossy image of me as a rock star. I think the pop star vanishes very quickly when people see the film. They just forget about Sting. I hope they do, that's the intention."

In a 1983 *Rolling Stone* interview Sting went one further in paralleling Martin to himself. "On one hand I'm a morose, doom-laden person, and on the other a happy-go-lucky maniac. I am as ambiguous as Martin. I didn't have to delve too deeply into myself to excavate him, he's definitely an exaggerated version of me."

As multi-layered as Martin is, the script cleverly disguises his true identity. Is he merely a hustler lying his way into the household or a more darker evil? The film never lets on. The original 1976 text, published in *New Review*, described Martin's toenails as "very long, curling and claw-like," suggesting the cloven foot of the Devil himself. "The television play more clearly indicated that the young man was the Devil," Kenneth Trodd, the film's producer, explained. "You're not really sure in the movie, there is just this terrible feeling of an evil presence in this house."

Martin might also represent the guilty conscience of the injured girl's father, who has concealed the background of his daughter's accident: she found him on the floor of his office with a secretary and in distress ran out of the building headlong into the path of a car. Her rape by Martin at the film's conclusion restores her lost speech and memory and in so doing creates fresh torment for the couple. "We tried to give the impression that it wasn't the first time that he had actually made love to her," Sting said. "He'd been doing it all along. He just went over the top on that occasion and that trauma is what brings her out." This is one of the film's main messages, the idea that evil actions don't necessarily have evil consequences.

Brimstone And Treacle received its world première at the Montreal Film Festival in September 1982. *Screen International* reported that the most impressive display of star power at the festival was not inspired by a movie star but from rock idol Sting. His press conference was easily the best attended, and wherever he went journalists and screaming fans followed close behind. The film opened in Britain on September 8 with a gala première at the Classic Haymarket in London. Afterwards there was the obligatory party with Sting and other celebrities including Boy George and Bob Geldof.

The film itself attracted a mixed reception. *The Guardian* thought it too obviously adapted from television, "Even at a brisk 87 minutes the material seems over extended." *The Motion Picture Guide* was in awe of the picture calling it, "A psychological corker, the suspense is excruciating. It could well rank up there with Hitchcock."

For his first major screen role Sting received good notices. "Where the film comes alive is in the presence of Sting," said *Films And Filming*. "It is a measure of Sting's success in the part of Martin that despite the weakness of the story, the film fascinates its audience to the end." *Screen International* commented: "Sting gives an excellent performance, proving that his startling début in *Quadrophenia* was no flash in the pan."

Denholm Elliot, in the role of the father as in the television production said, "Sting's awfully good, like someone who's been acting for years."

Richard Loncraine, *Brimstone*'s director, made a revealing comment about the working relationship he enjoyed with the star. "He has an astonishing screen presence, a face that reflects good and evil at the same time. It was a fantastic experience directing him.

"He always knew his lines. Many rock stars of his success could have said they wanted the biggest dressing room. At Shepperton Studios there weren't three dressing rooms of equal size, so he said to give Joan Plowright and Denholm Elliot the best. He's not a fool. He knew that was correct. He knew Denholm and Joan had earned their wings. He hasn't and they could've eaten him for breakfast."

In its first London week *Brimstone* took £28,000, and continued an average to good run, though it did less well in the provinces. "I'm very proud of it," Sting concluded. "It's quirky, weird and unusual. I'm not sure it's going to be a box office smash, but then it isn't meant to compete with *Star Wars*."

Brimstone And Treacle was a milestone in Sting's acting career, for it was in the part of Martin that he claimed respectability from his film world peers. It also gave him his first solo hit, 'Spread A Little Happiness', an old thirties number. "It was ironic that it was a hit, as it went totally against the grain," he commented. "It's fun to be able to do that. But if I'd done that at the beginning I wouldn't have stood a chance."

The film's soundtrack included other Sting tracks: 'Only You', 'You Know I Had The Strangest Dream', 'Narration' and the title track. The Police also contributed with 'How Stupid Mr Bates', 'I Burn For You' and 'A Kind Of Loving'.

Sting also performed two songs, 'Tutti Frutti' and 'Need Your Love So Bad' for another film, *Party, Party* in 1982.

It was a year which established Sting as the most successful British rock artist to make the transition from vinyl to celluloid since David Bowie, a situation that remains unchanged today. He revealed why so many rock stars turn towards cinema. "It's always an opportunity that's given to you. People in the film industry see you making money so they think, well maybe if we put him in a film the same people who buy his records will go and see the movie. That's not true, but why turn these offers down. Most of us have a go, very few make it."

Sting has not only transferred his talents to the cinema screen, but he's also tackled television and the difficult medium of radio drama. All that remains is theatre. In 1979 he even expressed a desire to write a novel. "When I'm about 40, I'm not ready yet. I've tried before when I was younger but didn't even finish them. I wouldn't mind trying my hand at script writing or movie making either."

In 1981 Sting portrayed Helith, the Angel Of
Love, in David Rudkin's epic BBC film *Artemis
'81*. It was an unusual fantasy concerning an
ancient pagan relic stolen from a museum. Hywel
Bennett was Gideon, a young writer on the
paranormal who discovers the relic contains the
power to destroy the earth. The interesting cast
also included Ingrid Pitt and a young Daniel Day
Lewis. "When I first received the script it was
three phone books thick," Sting explained. "It
was a very convoluted narrative which worked
on several levels."

Filming began on March 1, 1981 in Nottingham
and the following day at a disused Derbyshire
quarry designed to resemble the landscape of an
alien planet. Sting returned on April 7 to begin
four days of hard location work in Suffolk and a
further three the following week at a power station
in North Wales. His scenes were completed on
April 23 at the Pebble Mill studios in Birmingham.
"It's very erudite and dense," Sting said of the
film. "Some would say pretentious. I don't know
what it's like, it's hard to tell. On-stage you get
instant feedback, but there's no audience on a film
set, no reaction. I find that scary."

Broadcast on December 29, 1981 on BBC1, it ran
an uninterrupted three hours and five minutes.
Critics the next day were unsure of their opinions.
The Guardian thought it was made with "great
skill, devotion, beauty and no mercy," and was
impressed with Sting's performance. "Though
doing nothing in particular, Sting takes direction
beautifully and glows with a perfectly natural
phosphorescence."

Sting discussed how he felt to *Films And Filming*
on the likelihood that he was used in *Artemis '81*
for novelty pop star effect. "I thought the project
as a whole was arcane and interesting enough for
me to play that role and not feel compromised. It

was astonishing for British Television that it actually came off. I didn't care if I was being manipulated or not, I wanted to be in it."

Sting's first three feature films had all been British and had all been cursed with low budgets.

"Because I'm fairly inexperienced as an actor, it would be foolish of me to take on more than I can chew. It's better for me to be in small, arty movies. If I come out in some 30 billion dollar fiasco that's the end. I'm in a dangerous position, walking the tightrope between music and cinema. If I fall halfway along, rock isn't going to welcome me back, the film world isn't either. Until you make that transition and your credibility is established, it's quite risky," he explained.

"I've sort of come in from the underside and played in films that were left of field. I was surprised *Brimstone And Treacle* was even screened in the USA, much less distributed. I don't want to use my name because it's an Albatross around my neck. Who wants to see String in a movie anyway, String never heard of him. I'm proud of being a rock musician, but when I'm in a film I want to act."

Ironically Sting's very next film turned out to be the multi-million dollar *Dune*, and it was a boost to his new-found credibility that he survived the furore it was eventually to cause.

CHAPTER NINE

SYNCHRONICITY

"I do my best work when I'm in pain and turmoil."

THE L ATTER half of 1982 was to prove the most punishing of Sting's professional life. In May his song 'Don't Stand So Close To Me' was used in a TV ad for Bodymist deodorant. Sting was understandably livid with Virgin, his music publishers who received £5,000 for licensing it. "It's awful that advert," he exclaimed. "It sucks, it stinks. Trouble is everybody assumes that it's me cashing in on the song."

Partly due to this, he and Miles Copeland took Virgin to court in July to try to win his songs back from the contract he'd signed with Branson's company in 1976, when still a struggling artist in Newcastle, open to exploitation.

To demonstrate to the court that he was indeed in financial distress at the time of the contract's signing, Sting read out his diaries from the period to the jury. One entry, written in June 1977 when the family had moved to London, was quite alarming: "Money or the lack of it has raised its ugly head again. Joe is so innocent and vulnerable – God please help us."

The case was finally settled out of court after two weeks to prevent legal costs, already reaching £300,000, from escalating further. The settlement stated that Sting's songs were to be returned to him within seven-and-a-half years. According to the original contract they would've remained Virgin's property until 50 years after his death. Virgin also agreed to pay an extra seven-and-a-half per cent royalty on all the songs going back to 1976. Both sides naturally claimed victory and there occurred a sharp exchange of views between Miles Copeland and Richard Branson, with a happy press delighted to report the row.

Sting made his feelings known when The Police topped the bill at a giant outdoor concert in Gateshead on July 31. After an encore of 'Don't Stand So Close To Me', he yelled out to the crowd, "I hate Bodymist, I think Virgin Records stink, I think the whole legal process stinks."

Simultaneously, as the British press gleefully pointed out, Sting's marriage to Frances Tomelty appeared to be over. He was now often seen in the company of actress Trudi Styler, and the paparazzi had a field day in August when the couple flew to attend a party in France held by arms dealer Adnan Khashoggi. On their return to London scuffles for pictures of them resulted in one photographer being injured. As a card carrying Amnesty International member, it was perhaps rather tactless of Sting to have attended such a function. He later defended his action in a 1985 interview for *The Face*. "I got this request and he sent a jet to pick us up to fly us to Monte Carlo. I was fascinated by this excess, this madness. And frankly if it was wrong for my public image, well tough."

Sting was evidently dangerously close to succumbing to the perils of superstardom and its accompanying clichéd behaviour, of acting the caricature rock star, an image he detested. But the pressure at this stage must have been enormous, and nor was it helped by the sour over-exposure he courted from the press. "They've been very, very vindictive. It seems so stupid to give me a full page in the *Express*, when there's a war going on in the world," he said. He also confessed to have been emotionally at the end of his tether after the court

case. "Spending every day in court, wasting time
. . . it took its toll."

In December Sting took the opportunity to
exorcise such demons when The Police went to
Montserrat to record what was to be their vinyl
swan-song. The result was 'Synchronicity', the
group's darkest yet finest album. The title derives
from the lessons of Jung and his idea of a collective
unconscious, which The Police as a unit had by
now become, it also explored coincidence and the
idea of two separate events running on a parallel
course. The best example of this is 'Synchronicity
II', the narrative suggesting that at the same time as
a monster rises from the depths of a Scottish lake,
the beast within a working class man who has
fallen prey to his environment, also appears, two
events linked not logically but symbolically.

The title track is followed by, 'Walking In Your
Footsteps', a song where premonitions of global
doom reign as man follows in the footsteps of the
dinosaurs to ultimate extinction; 'Oh My God', a
song that allegedly dates back to Sting's Last Exit
days; the frenzied paranoia of Summer's 'Mother'
and Copeland's 'Miss Gradenko'.

But it is side two where the heart of the album can
be found. The first three songs are painfully
personal. 'Every Breath You Take', a song Sting
wrote while staying at 'Goldeneye', the Jamaican
home of 007 creator Ian Fleming in March 1983, is
obviously culled from his feelings over the break-
up of his marriage. "That was written at a time of
awful personal anguish, and it was a great catharsis
for me to write that song," he said later. 'King Of
Pain', is an amalgam of images of hurt and sorrow,
outpourings of a heart under siege. 'Wrapped
Around Your Finger', the sister of 'Every Breath',
brings this trilogy of personal odysseys to a close,
leaving 'Tea In The Sahara', a haunting song
inspired by an old Arab fable disclosed in the book

The Sheltering Sky, to conclude the album on a note of mystery and distance.

The group were justifiably proud of their achievement and spoke freely about 'Synchronicity' at its press launch in May. "I'm very proud of this one," said Sting. "It took us a very long time to do and was the hardest album we've made." It was no secret that there had been tension in the band with strong, though nearly always music-orientated, arguments between Sting and Stewart occurring during tense moments. This was an acknowledged part of the group's strength. "I'll argue till the cows come home about something I believe in," says Sting. "This album went through all kinds of horrendous cogs and gears to come out, emotionally and technically, the way it did."

'Synchronicity' was released on June 10, 1983 and was unanimously declared their most accomplished work to date. The most perceptive review came from *Rolling Stone*, who awarded the LP four-and-a-half stars, half a mark away from classic status. "The big surprise here," wrote their reviewer, "is the explosive and bitter passion of Sting's songs. Vestiges of his earlier romanticism remain in the melodies, but in the lyrics, paranoia, cynicism and excruciating loneliness run rampant. The end of this bleak, brilliant safari into Sting's heart deposits us at the edge of a desert, searching skyward, our cups full of sand."

NME too were impressed, "This record implies that Sting will grow as chameleonic as that other white demigod of pop, Bowie. A performer of greatness taking risks. An album of real passion that is truly impossible to decipher."

By October 1983 'Synchronicity' had sold 11 million copies, and *Smash Hits* unearthed some other fascinating facts about the album's sales. Placed end to end they would match the distance from London to Tel Aviv in Israel. Piled on top of each other, the stack would be 23 miles high, almost five Mount Everests or 382 times the height of Big Ben.

The first fragment of 'Synchronicity' was released in the form of 'Every Breath You Take' in May. Arguably Sting's masterwork, this beautiful melody is surely his most popular composition. "The bastards wrote us off, but I knew I had this song, I knew it would be number one," he said later. Indeed it was a huge international hit, their biggest in America, topping the charts Stateside for weeks on end. Sting received a special award to mark one million plays of 'Every Breath' on American radio. "If you work it out," he said, "that's the equivalent of playing it non-stop for five years on end."

The accompanying video was another turning point for The Police. The rawness and fun of their previous promos, all directed by Derek Burbridge, gave way to the glossy images of top video makers Kevin Godley and Lol Creme, though the promo for 'Every Breath', filmed in black and white, was joyless and plain. The video for 'Wrapped Around Your Finger', the follow-up single released in August which reached number seven, possessed an almost gothic quality with Sting parading among a sea of candles, looking radiant and assured. But unquestionably the most audacious promo of their career was that for 'Synchronicity II', released in October. The bizarrely costumed band were presented amid a multi-layered junk yard of ripped metal scaffolding and flying debris. Sting here resembled Feyd, his character from the film *Dune*, even down to the psychotic stare, it was a powerful and hypnotic performance.

The summer of 1983 saw The Police at their artistic peak with America in the palm of their hand. MTV constantly showed retrospectives of their video

work, each track from 'Synchronicity' played
endlessly on car radios across the country and
mini-biographies of Sting were sandwiched
between movies on cable TV. Evidence of Police
fever in America was apparent at that year's
Grammy Awards where they won, among others,
best group and song of the year for 'Every Breath'.
'Synchronicity' stayed number one in the US
album charts for a staggering 17 weeks.

The climax to their triumphant summer tour was
surely the Shea Stadium concert on August 18. In
1965 The Beatles had played there to 55,000 fans.
That night The Police attracted a 70,000-strong
audience, and tickets at $18 were sold out in less
than five hours.

Sting talked to *Smash Hit*'s reporter Neil Tennant,
now enjoying success with The Pet Shop Boys,
about his feelings towards the concert. "It means a
lot to me. If you look at why I'm a musician it's
because of The Beatles. So to do what they did, to
stand where Lennon stood, is very emotional for
me, almost unbearable."

The gig was a tremendous success and the group
finished 1983 with British gigs throughout
December, climaxing on the last days of the
year at Wembley.

CHAPTER TEN

DUNE

"I'm doing this film because of David Lynch, and for no other reason."

STING | **S DEAD** . Like a discarded rag doll he lies on the ornate tile floor of the great hall on the planet Arrakis, a knife embedded in his throat. Suddenly his body is almost consumed by a self-willed earthquake brought on by his assailant Paul. As in all fairy tales, good has triumphed over evil. These events form the thrilling climax of *Dune*, a hand to hand confrontation between the psychotic Feyd, played by Sting, and the movie's protagonist Paul Atreides. It is Sting's most challenging scene and he takes full advantage of it, spitting out vengeful words at his opponent and moving well within the tight fight choreography. He took lessons from Kiyoshi Yamazaki, a Japanese martial arts expert who helped him to feign the dangerous knife skills needed. The scene is also his last, his five-week stint on the movie, begun in May 1983 is over, and he leaves for the relative calm of Police rehearsals for an up-coming American tour. "It has to be some kind of event," said Sting of the movie. "It could be appalling, it could also be brilliant. If anyone can pull it off it's Lynch. I have high hopes for it."

Dune, the literary masterwork of Frank Herbert, first appeared in the mid-sixties and soon became a cult novel among the psychedelic generation of optimists who found within its hefty text areas devoted to religion, philosophy, politics and a final literary metaphor of hope. Since its publication in 1965, various film makers have attempted to transfer it to celluloid. Arthur P.Jacobs, the

producer of *The Planet Of The Apes* saga was
interested, as were Roger Corman and Ridley
Scott. Alejandro Jodorowsky, the surrealist,
went so far as to lavish a million dollars on
pre-production, and even hired Salvador Dali
as production designer. And America's Haskell
Wexler, who worked on The Rolling Stone's
film *Gimme Shelter*, hired a cast that included
Patrick McGoohan.

Dino De Laurentiis bought the rights in 1976, but
it wasn't until March 30, 1983 that cameras actually
began to roll. The choice of David Lynch as
director was made by De Laurentiis' daughter
Raffaella, the film's producer, after she had seen
The Elephant Man. "There's so much heart in that
movie," she said. "I don't cry in cinemas, I'm
tough. But I had tears in my eyes several times
during that one."

Unfamiliar with Herbert's novel, Lynch thought
Raffaella wanted to make a summer movie called
June, but after reading the book he realised the
awesome task ahead. *Dune* is renowned for its
complex plot, subplots and interweaving
characters. It concerns a young prince called Paul,
whose destiny it is to be the saviour of a planet
called Arrakis, sole supplier of a substance known
as 'Spice', which gives its masters untold powers.
Guarded by giant worms, other races will stop at
nothing to conquer its secrets and see Paul and his
royal family dead. The movie's plot is inevitably
different from the book, but Lynch tries to answer
some of the puzzles the novel sets by translating
them on to the screen in an altered form. "I didn't
want to pervert," he said. "Just to explain."

With a script completed, actors had to be found to
breathe life into the myriad of different characters
Herbert's imagination had spawned. These
included Max Von Sydow and Francesca Annis,
and Sting who played Feyd, nephew of Baron

Harkonnen, the leader of the villains. "He's a homosexual killer with a huge codpiece," Sting jokingly explained. "I really act it up." The role can be seen as an extension of his last part, the demonic Martin in *Brimstone And Treacle*. "I am Feyd," Sting confessed. "I honestly didn't have to do any preparation. He was Martin Taylor in a space suit. "This was certainly proof enough of the 'prince of darkness' tag that the press had hung on Sting during this period.

"He could be a very successful actor," mused a Hollywood insider in the November issue of *Esquire*. "The only thing that may limit him is his own taste, he always wants to play the dark prince. He's terrific at it, but really how many times can you play it?" Sting has explained his fascination with villainous characters. "I'm very lucky that I can exorcise my shadow, my demon on screen. Most people have to repress any dark shadow that they have, I'm allowed to bring it out."

The part of Feyd was won by Sting as a result of his performance in *Brimstone And Treacle*. "But I didn't really want to do the movie," he admitted. "As I didn't think it was wise for me to be in an enormous production." He had already turned down the chance to star as Fletcher Christian in Laurentiis' other 1984 film *The Bounty*. The part eventually went to Mel Gibson. But when Sting realised Lynch was to direct the *Dune* project he changed his views. "I really chose the director, I liked his past work, especially *Eraserhead*, though I still don't want to make movies just for the sake of being in them."

England, Tunisia, India and Italy were all considered as likely locations to shoot the mammoth picture. Churubusco studios in Mexico with its huge sound stages and nearby desert eventually proved the ideal choice, despite production difficulties stemming from Mexico's backward technology. Sting had other problems. "I had quite a few tapes stolen," he told Ed Naha for the book *The Making Of Dune*. "I had modified a bunch of computers to play music and I had all this digital information on cassette tapes. They got lost in customs. God knows what happened to them. When you play the tapes back over regular speakers it sounds like pigs grunting. I was pretty angry about it. The tapes took days of work to duplicate."

Mexico's location also accounted for personal dilemmas among cast and crew. The food was the main enemy and an Italian chef was flown in from New York accompanied by generous quantities of pasta. Filming in the desert led to many cases of sunstroke and fainting attacks. Imagine hell on earth, a rocky and arid place of lava formations almost eclipsed by two ominous volcanoes, a place where the poor of Mexico city dump their rubbish and unwanted dogs.

"I liked being on the planet Arrakis," Sting summed up. "But I could've lived quite nicely without the planet Mexico. The smog, the altitude and the food all conspire against you. This is the dirtiest job I've ever had and that includes construction work."

There were also several accidents which caused great concern among the team. Jimmy Devis, a unit director, broke his back during an evening shoot and Jurgen Prochnow, one of the film's many international stars, received second degree burns when a five kilowatt bulb exploded and sprayed hot glass across the set. "That was one of the most frightening experiences of my life," said Sting after the incident. "Jurgen was almost killed. I was right next to him, it was chilling, there was glass flying all over."

With cast and crew working under such horrendous conditions, there would have been few unhappy faces when on September 9, 1983 principal photography ceased. But there were still four hundred state-of-the-art special effects to be completed in under five months. The most challenging, the huge worms which inhabit Dune were the job of *ET* creator Carlo Rambaldi who built 16 worm models of various sizes. For close-ups a large section of worm was constructed, part of which was made with thousands of condoms. "Boy did that order look good being sent down here," joked Lynch. "What a manly movie." When all was finished the rough cut of the film lasted four hours. Lynch was not happy at the prospect of editing the huge movie, as for some time he had been working on a script for two sequels based on Frank Herbert's later *Dune* novels. The director hoped to make them back to back during 1985/86.

His dream never materialised as *Dune* was not the hit everyone connected with the film hoped it would be. Because the budget was so high, around 40 million dollars, it needed to recoup at least 100 million at the box office to be considered a success. It got nowhere near. It opened on December 13, 1984 with a London charity première at the Empire Leicester Square, attended by Prince Andrew and members of the cast, including Sting. In its first week the film took an excellent £60,126, but it soon ran out of steam, ending up a poor 21 in 1985's UK top money makers. In America it pulled a good $2,145,500 in seven days playing in 16 cities, but ended up with a sad total gross of only 14 million dollars by January 1986.

The critics were unmoved. The majority, although awed by the sheer scope of the picture, pointed to its major flaw, a reliance on the viewer already having some knowledge of the story. *The Monthly*

Film Bulletin summed up the problem: "*Dune* opens with a lecture concerning the characters and the significance of 'Spice' which succeeds in getting us nicely confused even before the opening credits. It's not easy either, despite diagrams, to grasp at speed who belongs to which planet. We flounder from one exchange to another throughout the film, hoping we've understood what we've heard."

Smash Hits were more blunt. "You need a degree in metaphysics to make head or tail of it," they joked. *The Guardian* thought it visually majestic but ultimately long and slow, while *Films And Filming* linked it with fifties' epics like *Ben Hur* and applauded Lynch's sense of directional grandeur. But others thought it a disaster of the very first order. This was a touch harsh as *Dune* was anything but a disaster, and considering it was only the third film Lynch had made, and his first in colour, it is a creditable achievement. Only in financial terms was *Dune* a complete failure.

Sting came out of it relatively unscathed. His role, though small, was just enough to linger in the memory, in particular in a scene in which he appears from a cloud of steam wearing only a codpiece. Originally he wanted to play the scene naked, which would have been interesting as this pose became the photograph most used for publicity purposes.

Sting was satisfied with the experience. "It was a good career move for me to be in an American film," he said. "Because no matter how much work you do in films in England, Hollywood still considers it small-time."

When the picture was released, merchandise flooded the market. A range of dolls appeared, including one of Sting. "My kids have one and throw it around the room," he said. "But it's not me, as a celebrity I'm open to all kinds of abuse."

In 1983 Sting was offered the role of Pontius Pilate in Martin Scorsese's *The Passion*. "I'd give my eye teeth to work with Scorsese," he declared. In November he screen tested and won the part. Unfortunately prior commitments ruled this out and David Bowie was cast in the part. When in 1988 it was released as *The Last Temptation Of Christ* it caused outrage and storms of protest in America and elsewhere.

As for *Dune*, when it received its television première in the same year over two consecutive nights, it had been entirely re-edited and now ran 50 minutes longer. Lynch, feeling it was no longer his work, had his name removed from the credits. For all the wrong reasons, *Dune* still remains Sting's most renowned film.

Sting later turned up on BBC2, playing Machiavelli in a dramatised documentary entitled *Ligmalion*, part of the *Arena* series. But it was in 1984 that he landed his favourite role, Mervyn Peake's dark hero Steerpike, the central character of *Titus Groan*, the first in a trio of novels called *The Gormenghast Trilogy*. These books, though not internationally known, are cult reading and their author is regarded by many as an undiscovered genius.

Sting became familiar with them when he was a trainee teacher after a girlfriend gave him them as a present. When he first tried to read the books he gave up after only a few chapters. "I was put off by the acres of dense language," he confessed. "A year later he fell under their spell and is now a confirmed addict. "They are so seductive, you start to live inside them. I ended up reading the entire trilogy in a week." His fanaticism is now considerable and he even called both his dog and horse Steerpike.

Sting bought the film rights for the novels and wrote a script with an eye on casting himself in the

lead if it ever came off. While attending The
Montreal Film Festival in 1982, he talked about the
project. "I'm trying to find a very good director to
work with. I may eventually try directing myself."
Sadly this now seems unlikely, but when he was
offered the role of Steerpike in a Radio 4
production of the first two books he leapt at it.
"It's a challenge I'm looking forward to," he
declared. "I've always been a fan of radio plays.
I have a great collection of the Sherlock Holmes
radio series on record."
It is easy to see why Sting identifies with Steerpike
so enthusiastically, as both of them are very alike.
In the book Steerpike manages to escape his menial
position in life to reach the top by a combination
of stealth and smooth charm, not dissimilar to
Sting's own rise from Newcastle obscurity to
world fame as a rock star. It is uncanny that a
drawing by Mervyn Peake of Steerpike on his
original manuscript circa 1946, strikingly resembles
Sting in appearance. Today though Sting has
relinquished the rights to the trilogy, after
auditioning Coppola and Scorsese as possible
directors. "I'm too old to play Steerpike. Once I'd
written the script and we'd done it as a radio play
I'd got it out of my system."
Titus Groan was broadcast on Radio 4 on
December 10, followed a week later by a
production of the second book *Gormenghast*.
Sting appeared in both versions. His performance
was praised by the *Daily Mail*, "Sting, who is
immediately more famous for being a rock star is
also a good actor. He shows himself in this to have
the exact vocal presence for his part and to possess
the power to make the malevolent heart of the dark
drama glow with eerie precision."
To this day it remains his most diverse work, and
in the words of the *Radio Times* who featured

Sting on their cover for that week, he was now unquestionably 'a star at his Peake'.

CHAPTER ELEVEN

DREAM OF THE BLUE TURTLES

"I haven't left The Police. I'm just exploring different areas with other musicians."

DREAMS COME IN many shapes and forms. This particular dream focuses the subconscious on a typical English garden, with delicate rose beds, immaculate lawn and ivy covered stone wall around the perimeter to prevent prying eyes from looking within. Soon the serenity is broken by the arrival of large blue turtles. Once inside they begin wrecking the orderly garden.

When Sting had that very dream he knew exactly what it meant and his Jungian teachings had taught him to use dreams creatively. The turtles represented his new band and the destruction of his neat garden was an obvious denouncement of how easy his life and options had become. "I had that dream at a time when I had doubts about my future," he said. "Should I stay with The Police and make a safe album ? The dream said no."

Sting's decision to go solo came at a time of increasing speculation over The Police as a viable, working unit. At the end of 1983, which had seen an American tour rake in millions, 'Synchronicity' was hailed as their finest work. Fans were shocked when the group announced 1984 would be a rest year, and magazines around the world cashed in on speculative stories of rifts within the band. Rumours of a Police split, strongly denied with less conviction each time by Stewart Copeland, grew yet more thunderous when the group took legal action over a *Daily Mail* article claiming the band had split up. It was a sure sign that things were bad and the excuse of a sabbatical to pursue solo projects seemed more hollow now than ever. During the split rumours Sting remained fairly silent. Proving that action speaks louder than words, he held court in New York in January 1985, setting up a three-week workshop with an open invitation to members of the jazz community to come along and jam, the idea being to pick the cream to play on his début solo album. "I was astounded by the names that came through the door," he said. "People whose records I'd learnt from."

Despite the rumours of a rift, The Police turned up at the annual British Phonographic Industry Awards in February. On national television they were seen collecting a major achievement award, but unbeknown to the audience, behind the group's jovial exterior and antics which included mocking the award's presenter, an A&M bigwig, there were no plans for a reunion or a new album. Apparently they owed A&M another LP, which many believed would be a live album, an idea which was eventually shelved. 1986 saw the release of a greatest hits compilation, a commercial cop out perhaps, but it did contain a brilliant reworking of 'Don't Stand So Close To Me'. Released as a single it only reached number 24, but it was complemented by a beautifully nostalgic video. The initial idea had been to re-record all their hit singles. In 1983 Sting discussed the idea with *NME*: "An idea I've had for a while is instead of releasing a greatest hits album, is to record them again, improve them, make them more contemporary."

Meanwhile Sting had formed his new band: Omar Hakim from Weather Report on drums, Darryl Jones of Miles Davis' band on bass, Branford Marsalis on sax, Kenny Kirkland on keyboards with Sting himself on a subdued rhythm guitar. All this was a half-deliberate return to his pre-Police jazz days in Newcastle. "I suppose this is the Last Exit of my dreams," he confessed referring to his old jazz band. Even songs like 'I Burn For You' and 'Low Life' from those early years would be utilised in the forthcoming tour.

On February 25 the freshly assembled band made their first live appearance at the Ritz Club in New York. Police favourites like 'Roxanne' were performed alongside such jazz classics as 'Been Down So Long'. Sting also sang 'Children's Crusade', 'We Work The Black Seam Together' and 'If You Love Somebody Set Them Free' for the first time. The concert was a resounding success and before flying to Barbados to start recording the album at Eddie Grant's 'Blue Wave' studios, there were two other gigs at a downtown Manhattan club.

'I've spent too many years at war with myself', is a line from 'Consider Me Gone' one of the tracks off the album and proof of a definite change in Sting's life, both artistically and personally. With 'Dream Of The Blue Turtles', he focused his songwriting talent on the troubled world outside, leaving his inner turmoil, at its height between autumn 1981 and the end of 1982, which he refers to as 'The Fall', on the sidelines. He concentrates here on world issues, a myriad of which are tackled with deft lyrical skill, be it world peace, nuclear power and weapons or love politics. This is not to say that such concerns weren't raised on Police records; they were, most notably on the last two. But on this LP they take the driving seat, perhaps because Sting has matured as a human being and artist with as big a stake in the future as any of us: four children he would like to see grow up in a peaceful and unpolluted world. Sections of the press unfairly linked this maturing to a selfish desire to become a more dignified rock star archetype; but

this was a brave and vulnerable time for Sting.
He could have made a Police album and cleaned
up, but he chose to expose himself to challenge
and criticism.
The songs presented on the new album were
gathered over a two-year period and then groomed
before actual recording. Sting's method was to
perform the songs himself on a demo tape, then
let the band collect ideas and flesh out the tape
until it resembled a solid piece of music. In this
way the album was completed in an extraordinarily
short time.
During the recording of the album, Sting's son Joe
joined him on the chorus of one of the songs. Sting
with his arms around him and eyes closed missed
what sent the control room into hysterics. Joe was
giving an amazing impression of his dad as a pop
star. "He did that, my Joe!" Sting exclaimed. "I
can handle the bloody critics, but lampooned by
my own son."
It was during this trip to the Caribbean that Sting
almost lost his life while deep sea diving, when he
suddenly ran out of air hundreds of feet below the
ocean. Swimming to the surface from that depth
would have been fatal, and so he swam parallel to
the sea floor to reach his instructor and sharing her
tank they surfaced together.
'If You Love Somebody Set Them Free' opens the
album, a fast, catchy tune and arguably the most
commercial song on the LP. Sting saw it as an
antidote to 'Every Breath You Take', which he
now viewed as an evil song about possessing an
individual for selfish gains. It was the obvious
teaser single but only reached number 26, though
in America it was a top five hit. Its poor run in
Britain may have been due to a rather uninspired
video which presented the new band in a dull light,
performing in one room for the entire length of the
promo. But the remaining singles also fared badly

in the UK charts, despite being popular in America. When the album was released on June 17 1985 it did well on both sides of the Atlantic, a number three in the UK and six weeks at number two in America.

According to popular myth the seventh wave that breaks on any shore is the strongest, the most profound. In 'Love Is The Seventh Wave', the album's second track, Sting imagines the world drowning amid a wave of nuclear weapons and armies ever ready for war. But the lyric also promises hope in the form of a future wave of peace, one of the album's recurring themes. Writing about personal beliefs and concerns is not new but since the *Live Aid* concert rock music has showed the world that it can force some kind of change, and Sting is at the forefront of this movement. His self-effacing humour is glimpsed at the song's close when he sings a few joke lines from 'Every Breath' – 'Every cake you bake, every leg you break.' Released as a follow-up to 'Love Somebody' it fared even worse, reaching only a poor 41.

'Russians', arguably the best track on the album, is unquestionably one of Sting's finest compositions. Haunting, powerful and stitched together from a stolen Prokofiev melody, it became, at number 12, the highest charting single from the album. A&M had wanted the song to be the second single from the album, "but I didn't want to bum people out during the summer," Sting told *Playboy*, "so I waited for nearer winter."

Originally he wanted to record the song with a Russian orchestra, an attempt at making personal contact with musicians from the other side of the Iron Curtain, however red tape eventually blocked the plan.

One of Sting's children sowed the seed for the song by asking his father if there was a bomb that could destroy the world. "Children feed my anger," he said. "They're completely innocent. The older I get the more bitter I become."

Before recording 'Russians', he spent a morning with the head of Soviet Studies at Columbia University watching Russian television via satellite, in order to witness Soviet life at first hand.

The theme of innocent children is also explored in 'Children's Crusade', a title which echoes back to an 11th century crusade in which European children were recruited, only to be sold off for slavery, although Sting never mentions this atrocity in the song. Instead the bulk of the lyric concentrates on the First World War, when boy soldiers, 'virgins with rifles', were sent to France for cannon fodder, an entire generation betrayed and butchered. The poppy has since become the symbol of their remembrance, and Sting uses the floral image as a parallel to the horrors of heroin addiction today. More young lives wasted.

"The song isn't an attack on addicts," he told *Record Mirror*. "But the fat businessmen who make all the profits. They are the same breed who sold those children into slavery or sent people off to fight in the 1914-18 war. I wish them hell."

Like 'Russians', the song showcases a new mature performer, not so much the rock star as an anxious parent.

Where 'Russians' addressed world topics, 'We Work The Black Seam', which opens side two, proves that Sting is also aware of the importance of home grown issues. He was careful to point out that the song did not defend the miners' strike, but was a tribute to miners themselves. It expressed support for coal as a source of energy as opposed to the dangerous alternative of nuclear power. He had first hand knowledge of this subject: not only did he grow up in a mining community but he also taught many miners' children at a school in

Northumberland. "I'm writing idealistic songs, hopeful ones, because we need to be that in order to win a future worth having," he said.

'Consider Me Gone', another haunting melody, reflects Brechtian influences. Like the German songwriter who wrote both friendly and unfriendly songs, Sting has his humanitarian compositions which ask for world peace, one world. But he also has his mean selfish songs like Brecht, of which 'Consider Me Gone' features prominently. There are echoes of a split persona here.

The penultimate song 'Moon Over Bourbon Street' was inspired by Ann Rice's book *Interview With A Vampire*. Set in New Orleans, where Sting apparently wrote the song under a genuine full moon, it concerns a man who has become a vampire by accident and whose conscience is troubled over his need to kill to stay alive. The duality of man attracted Sting to this idea, and his ongoing fascination with the dark side of men, those who are both Devil and angel. As a single it barely made the top 50.

The last track, 'Fortress Around My Heart', is one of the few songs that The Police could perform comfortably. Indeed Sting had used an old Police song 'Shadows In The Rain', from 'Zenyatta Mondatta' to close the previous side. It also harked back to 'Every Breath You Take'. "It's an image of a structure around a person, ostensibly to protect them but ultimately to control them; so much so that you end up isolated from them. Again an antidote song," he explained.

The unveiling of the album took place in Paris, with a press conference followed by a series of concerts at the small Mogador Theatre. In the midst of all this Sting's girlfriend Trudy Styler gave birth to his fourth child, a boy they named Jake. "A new band, a new album and a new baby all at the same time," he observed. "I call that auspicious."

During this period Sting's every move was not only scrutinised in articles for various global rock journals, but also by a movie crew who were filming events for posterity. They had plenty of material, including a gem from one of the Mogador shows, when a small pink castle with a cardboard heart stuck on it was lowered to the stage at the end of 'Fortress'. . . a road crew joke. "At least it wasn't Stonehenge," commented Sting. He'd seen *Spinal Tap* too.

After Paris, with the album safely launched, a world tour took in Japan, America, Canada and Europe, and finally hit Britain with showcase performances at The Royal Albert Hall in January. The shows included plenty of tracks from the new LP together with a handful of Police songs including 'Driven To Tears', and a cappella versions of 'Roxanne' and 'Message In A Bottle'. Midway through the tour Sting fulfilled a lifetime ambition to appear on a Miles Davis album, although all he did was shout the Miranda rights (what American policemen say to suspects during arrest) into a microphone. "At the end he said, 'Great to meet you Sting, see you around.'That was Miles Davis, 10 minutes, a great character."

Into the American run of the tour it was evident that Sting's serious Police image had given way to a happier exterior. There was certainly much good humour among the band members for this was no series of sombre jazz concerts intent on educating rather entertaining audiences. "I think I'm funnier now," Sting revealed. "Someone threw a bra on-stage the other night. I said . . . 'look those new Sony Walkman headsets have arrived'."

In the 'Turtle' band Sting's role was very clearly defined. Even though he was the leader it was still very much a group, not just Sting and a bunch of backing musicians. Though the set-up did have its detractors. "The band are much better at playing than I am, but I'm better at conceptualising," Sting explained. "All the roles are very well defined, whereas in The Police it wasn't often clear." 'Dream Of The Blue Turtles' was a critical and commercial triumph, and was seen as the final nail in the coffin for The Police. "In that group I was just a robot, with very Aryan type energy. I was terrible to work with or to be around. I was a complete nightmare, unsympathetic, aggressive, mean, selfish, egotistical. But so were the others." Sting was now truly on his own.

CHAPTER TWELVE

THE BRIDE — PLENTY

"It was a great script, a very clever idea. I get killed again, as usual, and don't get the girl."

1985 **P**ROVED to be Sting's most spectacular year to date. Not only was his first solo album released, but he was also involved in two feature films that were later released within a month of each other. *The Bride* reunited Sting with Franc Roddam, the man who gave him his first screen acting role in *Quadrophenia*.

Roddam was careful to point out during the release of *The Bride*, that it wasn't a re-make of James Whale's classic *Bride Of Frankenstein* but a personal telling of the story. "It takes off from the Mary Shelley novel in an entirely different direction from the 1935 film," he said. "My film is more of a fairy tale, but I'm filming it as if it were *All The President's Men*."

The most immediate difference between the two films is that Roddam's bride is conceived at the beginning, whereas in Whale's production her creation was left to the last thrilling moment. The film opens, like all good Gothic horror tales, in a dark brooding castle amid the roar of a thunderstorm. It is here that Frankenstein, in the movie's only truly horrifying sequence, creates a mate for his monster who waits eagerly in the catacombs below. The unveiling of the bride, the angelic and fragile Jennifer Beals, leads only to disaster when in a rage the monster destroys the laboratory.

These opening scenes fondly recall those Hammer horror pictures, it reeks of cliché, but works wonderfully, even down to the hunchback

assistant thrown in among all the electrical
paraphernalia and thunderclaps. Frankenstein's
other helper, Dr Zahlus is played by Quentin
Crisp, the brilliant raconteur and later the subject
of Sting's song 'An Englishman In New York'. He
is killed in the castle fire, but the Baron and his
creation, whom he calls Eva, manage to escape.
As the often misunderstood Frankenstein, Sting
physically fits the role like a glove although
originally he wasn't set to play the Baron who,
because of Peter Cushing's definitive portrayal, is
generally regarded as being an older man. Mary
Shelley however, made it obvious in her book that
Frankenstein was 32, roughly Sting's age.
"I did it primarily as a challenge, to make the
audience sympathise with a person that in the past
has carried a bad name," he said. In *The Guardian*
he further elaborated on his liking for characters
with the capacity for both bad and good.
"I feel Frankenstein has the potential for good and
the necessary evil the plot requires. I also see him
as a frustrated widower, who creates a woman he
can control in order to bridge his loneliness." This
is one of the film's main themes for as Sting
educates Eva, turning her into a scholarly lady,
almost his own Eliza Dolittle, he is in fact creating
a mate not for his monster but one for himself.
During filming Sting was romantically linked with
Miss Beals. "Apparently we got married
somewhere in the South of France," Sting
commented. "I don't remember the ceremony, but
it must be true, it was in the *Daily Mail*."
Reviews were mostly negative. *Films And Filming*
called it . . . "A muddled mixture of modern
manners in a Regency Europe culled from the
pages of Georgette Heyer instead of Mary
Shelley," and described Sting as, "a moist fag end."
Variety said, "In opting to tone down the horror
aspects of the genre to fit in with the film's fairy

tale aura, they have made a Frankenstein film that's not scary." Only *Film Review* offered hope by saying that if the film had been produced 50 years ago it would now be an established classic. Perhaps *The Guardian* was the most accurate in wondering if such a curious hybrid would work well with modern audiences. The question should have been whether the public really wanted to see another version of the Frankenstein legend, and after Mel Brooks brilliant 1974 send up, would another serious attempt at the myth hold up? This turned out to be the case, and *The Bride* was a financial disaster. Released in Britain on November 1 1985, it took only £12,000 in its first week at the Odeon Leicester Square. In America it barely made a million and a half dollars in a fortnight.

Much of the criticism heaped on *The Bride* was only marginally justified. Being a romanticised version of a legendary story it left itself open to ridicule, but the film's biggest flaw was its lack of any genuine horror and suspense. Roddam had deliberately made an anti-horror movie. "It's not your average terror film," he said. "And once you get past the first 10 minutes it isn't even a science movie. If you accept the basic conventions of this type of picture, as you accept the convent ions of a movie like *Star Wars*, it becomes just a film about people."

"It wasn't a good movie," Sting later admitted. "But I thought I was quite good. I had to act a lot. Many things went wrong on that film. It was camp because it took itself too seriously. The problem was that I was the most experienced actor in the cast and normally I work with experienced performers who bolster you up. It was hard."

Concurrent with *The Bride*'s release, Sting took part in a campaign by The American Library Association, to encourage reading literacy. In his *Bride* costume, he was photographed sitting on a wall in front of a looming castle reading a book. This ad appeared in numerous periodicals and in poster form in libraries across the country. "Teaching is a positive and useful thing in an age of brutality and sub-literacy," he said. "I really believe in reading, otherwise I'd be reading *The Sun* every day like my peers and thinking I was getting the news."

While *The Bride* collected negative reviews from critics, *Plenty* which opened a few weeks later, promptly found instant favour and almost unanimous approval. Originally a stage play, David Hare's *Plenty* premièred at London's National Theatre in 1978 with Kate Nelligan as Susan, the role taken by Meryl Streep in the film, and was written in Hare's own words, "out of white hot anger with England." After a Broadway run it was swept up by two American producers and turned into a crafted, stylish but ultimately downbeat vision of Britain's post-war decline through the eyes of a woman, whose views and attitudes are the self-confessed echoes of the author himself.

Hare adapted his own play for the screen and during post production removed some of the distractions of the original text. It remains a biting indictment of a nation's lost opportunities, and the effect of a crumbling Empire on society's losing battle for a prosperous future with 'plenty' for all. However, its thoughts on the absurdity and priggishness of class division need more savage insight.

As Susan, Meryl Streep is superb, confirming her status as the finest screen actress of her generation. Sting is also commendable as a Cockney lad who is cruelly rejected by her after being unable to produce a child. Sting first appears, not surprisingly, in a jazz club, and though he has few scenes he radiates an assured sexuality throughout,

notably in his love scene with Streep. "A whole afternoon we were, like, making love," he quipped. "I kept thinking, 'God I'm getting paid for this'."
In an *NME* interview close to the picture's release, Sting discussed his feelings towards movie acting: "I don't really want to be an actor, it's not my vocation. I do it, one because I'm asked and two because I enjoy it. I like the idea of getting out of bed at six in the morning looking like shit. There's nothing glamorous about making films. I can't go on a film set and say, 'Here I am, God's gift to acting, big rock star, I sell millions of records.' It doesn't mean shit, if anything it's a disadvantage. When I go to do a film, I'm learning to act, and as soon as people have realised that I'm not some drug-taking egomaniac, I usually get on very well, learn a lot and come out unscathed."

Plenty opened in the last week of November. *Film Review* called it, "A triumph, crisp, intelligent and angry. An excellent realisation of a brilliant play." *Films And Filming* gave it three stars and said, "As a probing record of an apathetic Britain it left me irritated; as a chance to see some wonderful actors shown to excellent advantage, it is invigorating. Sting takes another assured step in his acting career. He's got a Cockney sexuality that doesn't seem to require a wardrobe to make the point, and an underlying sincerity that makes him believable." *The Times* however dismissed it as . . . "Calculated and stagey."

Speaking to *The Times* in 1986, Sting assessed his acting career to date. "It's been patchy, but I'm growing as a cinema performer all the time. I don't expect to be Hoffman or Olivier overnight. But every film I've done has been successful. I'm not at all disappointed."

CHAPTER THIRTEEN

BRING ON THE NIGHT

"I wanted an honest film, not a rock 'n' roll movie."

ON THE TOP FLOOR of the busy Pompidou Centre in Paris one hot Friday afternoon, journalists from all over Europe converged to record the prestigious unveiling of Sting's new band. The man himself looked tired, having spent the previous night at the hospital presiding over the birth of his new son, Jake. He now faced the less charitable task of keeping press hounds at bay, fencing off inevitable 'Have The Police split' questions while getting on with the job in hand, introducing his new band. Also in attendance were a film crew and top Hollywood director Michael Apted, overseeing the proceedings as part of a feature length film chronicling the conception, rehearsals and opening concert of Sting's solo tour. In true cinema fashion, Apted juggled with reality by using professional extras acting as journalists for one particular scene at the press conference. "I wanted to get a really striking shot of the whole thing," he told a real newspaper reporter. "And I couldn't trust you lot to get it right."

The idea behind the film was clearly determined by Sting. He wanted to make a rock documentary about the early stages of a group, as opposed to recording the events after the onset of fame. "I set the whole thing up to capture what it was like to start a band," he said. "This is about a new group of people coming together and trying to figure out how to arrange and play songs in a short space of time, and being filmed doing it. We eventually ran out of money and time, but that was the tension of the film."

Bring On The Night was financed by A&M's film division with a reported budget of over one million pounds. The choice of director for such an original venture was a problem that rested purely on Sting's shoulders. He spoke to such luminaries as Coppola and Scorsese, but instead chose a little known English director now residing in the US, Michael Apted.

Learning his craft in British television by directing episodes of *Coronation Street* and well over 50 plays, in recent years he'd moved into cinema, with *Gorky Park*, *Continental Divide* with John Belushi and in 1988 *Gorillas In The Mist*. But more important was *Stardust*, seen by many, including Sting, as the archetype British rock movie.

Apted was also responsible for a television series that focused on a group of people from differing social backgrounds at seven-year intervals. The most recent, *28 Up*, had caught Sting's attention, and he offered Apted the job. It was too good an offer to refuse, and he established an immediate rapport with Sting.

"I chose Michael because I wanted someone who could look at things with a more jaundiced eye and attempt to get behind the people involved," Sting told *The Times*. "Jake's birth happened during the film's schedule and Apted talked us into including it, as not to would have been a dishonest account of those nine days in my life. I don't think it's a piece of gratuitous home movie making. I think it's a moving and honest moment and I'm willing to take the rap." In the finished film the track 'Russians' plays over this sequence.

The director's approach to the picture was to involve the cinema audience in what was happening on screen as much as possible. Rock concert films are no substitute for the real thing, so the idea was to let the viewer in on the secrets of putting on a show, the pitfalls and sheer hard work of rehearsing, and a sense of the relationships that develop within a band.

For the most part the group are seen practising at the Château Du Courson, a majestic house set in the green meadows of France. One episode features a group of tourists being shown around the building, including Sting's rehearsal room during a run through of 'Shadows In The Rain'. Many put their fingers in their ears, while the guide has to shout out the items of interest to make himself understood above the noise. The second half of *Bring On The Night*, features the opening concert at the Mogador.

During the project Sting voiced strong misgivings. "I was panicking," he recalled. "We were really rehearsing, without enough time to do it and it seemed to me that the film-makers were recording a disaster taking place. I was terrified, exhausted. I was past caring how I looked, I simply couldn't deal with the camera." He even threw a couple of people off the set who were voicing similar fears. "It was stupid of me as all they were doing was speaking the truth. But that kind of negative attitude is deadly on a film set."

Apted on the other hand was full of praise for the way Sting handled the obvious pressure he was under. "He's enormously self-controlled and you felt he'd decided how much he was going to reveal in the film and how much he was going to hold back," Apted told *The Guardian*. "For him the whole experience was a kind of self-discovery because I think he knew very well this Prince of Darkness that he'd been portraying as part of The Police was over, and that he wanted to make himself more accessible, more appealing. And the album, the tour and the film are all part of that."

Sting was pleased with the finished result. Asked if
parts of the film made him cringe he replied, "Yes,
there are some bits that hurt, but at the end I think
I come out as a warmer person than many people
probably think I am."
Bring On The Night, released in June 1986,
attracted a mixed critical reaction. Some thought it
pretentious, while others declared it to be little
more than a glorified promo for Sting's new album.
But Leonard Maltin, American film historian and
critic called it, "a first rate musical documentary."
Financially the film proved a weighty
disappointment, but a live album, released as a tie-
in with the movie, had more success reaching
number 16 in the UK album charts.
In 1986 Sting's stated intention was to tackle a
'politically important' film. He was seriously
considering playing the part of a South African
doctor who was executed because of his links with
the anti-apartheid movement. Though the project
never materialised, Sting used the Nelson Mandela
concert of 1988 as a platform to express his anger at
the apartheid system by opening the proceedings
with 'If You Love Somebody Set Them Free'.

With the Bring On The Night tour
musicians at London's Royal Albert
Hall. *(Pictorial Press)*

Opposite, top:
With Russell Harty at the Grammy
Awards. *(Barry Plummer)*

Opposite, bottom:
With Bruce Springsteen during the
Human Rights Now Tour 1988. *(LFI)*

Opposite, top:
With Phil Collins at Live Aid
Concert, London, July 1985. *(LFI)*

Opposite, bottom:
With Human Rights Now Tour at
JFK Stadium, Philadelphia 1988.
L-R: Peter Gabriel, Tracey Chapman,
Youssou N'Dour, Sting, Joan Baez &
Bruce Springsteen. *(Pictorial Press)*

Above:
Promoting the 'I Ran The World'
fund raising event, May 1986.
(Andy Phillips)

Right:
At Wembley during Nelson Mandela
concert 1988. *(LFI)*

Left:
With fellow mods
in Quadrophenia.
(Brent Walker/NFA)

Below:
As Feyd in the film
'DUNE' in 1984.
(Universal/NFA)

Opposite, top:
With Meryl Streep
in 'Plenty'.
(Pictorial Press)

Opposite, bottom:
As the evil Martin Taylor
in the film 'Brimstone
And Treacle' 1982. *(NFA)*

CHAPTER FOURTEEN

NOTHING LIKE THE SUN

"I'm probably more romantic now than I used to be. I'm more comfortable with my own personality, but I'm still a bastard at times. As for the real me, that's my business, I'm changeable, I don't ever want to be consistent."

STING WON THE best British album category for 'Nothing Like The Sun', at the British Phonographic Industry Awards in February 1988, an acknowledgment from his fellow artists of his success since the demise of The Police, and a salute to a decade of songwriting.

Sting was on tour in America and unable to collect the award in person, but he video taped an acceptance speech on the night of a sell-out Madison Square Garden gig, five days before it would eventually by seen by millions of television viewers around the world.

"I was asked to make a short speech, so I decided to write something about Clause 28," he told *NME*. "I said that I was proud to accept the award because I was proud to be British, and one of the reasons why was that we generally treat our minorities reasonably well. I said I wanted to accept the award in a spirit of tolerance and under standing, a spirit that Clause 28 put under threat."

However brave it was of Sting to speak out on such a delicate subject, his efforts were in vain. When A&M bosses Herb Alpert and Jerry Moss presented the award to him all that was glimpsed was a hearty handshake and a brief thank you. The BBC, who transmitted the programme, and the BPI both shirked responsibility for the broadcasting of the speech, and when Sting was told the next day he commented, "I just hope it was a question of time."

Sting ran into deeper trouble with the song 'They Dance Alone', a tribute to the wives and mothers of political prisoners who in protest dance by themselves outside prisons or in public squares. It was met with fierce anger from the Chilean government, and both single and album were banned. When Sting was in Argentina towards the end of 1987, he met women who performed similar protests, and was almost arrested. "Playing Buenos Aires, where we had the mothers of the disappeared on stage with us, was pretty amazing," he said. When he played there again in October 1988 as part of the Amnesty tour, much the same thing occurred. "Security forces can't arrest you for dancing," Sting announced. "But this is such a powerful image . . . of women dancing with pictures of their loved ones pinned on their clothes instead of going out there with Molotov cocktails." This heart-rending image was utilised in the video for 'They Dance Alone'.

'Nothing Like The Sun', was recorded in Montserrat with only two musicians from the 'Turtles' album, Branford Marsalis and Kenny Kirkland. To compensate there was an impressive line-up of guest stars including Mark Knopfler, Eric Clapton, Gil Evans and Andy Summers. Sting wrote and prepared the majority of the album isolated in New York. "I'm not anti-social, but I tend to thrive creatively when I'm left alone. I just shut myself away for three months and wrote." During the recording of the album Sting suffered the first of what was to be a series of bereavements in a traumatic six months that claimed the lives of both his parents. In June he learned that his mother Audrey, who had bravely fought cancer for two years, was close to the end. He was unable to write a single note, such was the emotional blow. "Until she's out of pain, until she dies," he confided to a friend, "I can't really open up and be creative." When her final battle was lost, Sting declared, "It's all right now, she's not in pain any more."

Shortly after her death Sting wrote 'Lazarus Heart', as a tribute, so close was their relationship. His mother was the last person left who still called him Gordon. "I quite literally got music from my mother. One of my earliest memories is of sitting under the piano at her feet as she worked the pedals and played the piano. It was she who encouraged me to play the guitar and she was the one who listened to me." 'Nothing Like The Sun' was dedicated to his mother, a press release explained that she had been Sting's "maternal strength in the face of male-triggered social and political disaster."

Less than six months after his mother's death tragedy struck again when Sting's father died just before the official opening of his world tour in Rio De Janeiro. The first night was in the city's Marcana stadium, packed to capacity, an incredible 200,000 people. "I walked on-stage in front of all those people and felt like I had to celebrate him," he told *The Sunday Mirror*. "It was a wake for me, so it was kind of joyous. One of the sadnesses is that the gig was a confirmation of beingness and my parents were dead. At the same time I felt very strongly that they were with me in a way."

Sting did not attend either of his parents' funerals, rightly realising that by doing so he would create a media circus. "That's no way of grieving for somebody, and rather than go and spend some time with a family I'm not really close to I worked instead. I just thought this was a better way of doing it. It was a better tribute. Life goes on."

Sting once said that one of the reasons he became a performer was to get attention from his mother and father. "And the ultimate kind of attention

you can receive is to become a celebrity. My
parents had to take notice of me then."

As a final blow Gil Evans, who played on the
album and was a close friend of Sting, also died. In
order to rise above the shock and grief of recent
events, Sting retreated into himself and from public
scrutiny, but in doing so attracted criticism for
becoming an island. In an unexpected move Sting
replied to his critics through the letter pages of
their respective journals, which inspired an essay in
The New York Times telling him not to be so thick
skinned. "I have thick skin," Sting told *Hello*
magazine. "I've been in this business too long not
to develop it. I've been called everything,
talentless, pretentious. Personally I'd really like to
be spiteful back. It's only human. Maybe I am
pretentious and arrogant, but people forget how
much courage it takes to perform in front of 20,000
and entertain them for three hours."

The pretentious label is one which Sting has always
had to live with, and following his recent solo
musical leanings he has also been charged with
being a dilettante. He defended the accusation in
NME. "People keep telling me that what I'm
playing isn't jazz. I know it's not jazz. My music is
structured and arranged, there's a very rigid
discipline which I impose, but within that the
musicians are allowed to paint their own colours.
I'm not trying to play jazz or rip off black music.
I think it's one thing appealing to a cult minority,
but quite another reaching a broad spectrum of
people. It's pretty sophisticated music, and to me
the idea of a 12-year-old listening to these
musicians represents victory. I can live with the
praise and the blame."

'Nothing Like The Sun', was released in October
1987 and widely acclaimed as a masterpiece. The
English music press – as a matter of course –
received it less enthusiastically, with *Melody*

Maker's Steve Sutherland calling it the most pretentious record he'd ever encountered. The *NME* was more constructive. "It's a richer album than 'Dream', but very much a sequel. Generally he seems more at ease and 'Straight To My Heart' even recalls 'Synchronicity', suggesting, as does the presence of Andy Summers on two songs, that he's come far enough on from that band not to have to keep an unnatural distance from what is after all a part of himself."

The album produced three singles, hits in other countries but, as in the case of the 'Turtle' releases, failures in the UK charts. "Sting is about as interesting as compact discs. This song is almost bad enough to be Robert Palmer," is how *NME* described the first, 'We'll Be Together'. It was hardly surprising that with this kind of negative attitude and negligible radio play the single hardly surfaced in the charts.

In the days of The Police, Sting was very conscious of the music charts and could, when called upon, disclose not only where the band stood in the top 40 but any other group too. "I remember every number one there's ever been, I could sing a verse of it. It's a good feeling to be part of all that." Recent less than charitable remarks however, concerning pop, Radio One and the charts in general, suggest that this interest may have mellowed with maturity. But thoughts on the commercial aspects of the system still taunt: "Sell 17,000 singles in Britain and you get more recognition than if you sell half a million albums." The follow-up, 'An Englishman In New York', was more of an open tribute to Quentin Crisp. The pair had met when Sting suggested him for a role in *The Bride*, and their friendship grew when Sting came to New York. "He's one of my heroes and one of the most courageous men I've ever met. He was homosexual in England at a time when being

so was physically dangerous, and he was himself,
with no apologies, in such a flamboyant and brave
way that should be an example to us all."
'Englishman In New York' was used in the film
Stars And Bars, in which an English gent loses
himself among the indulgence of American society.
Sting also performed the theme for the popular
1988 thriller *Someone To Watch Over Me*.
Nothing Like The Sun, topped the charts across the
world, including Britain and America. Following
hard on its success Sting embarked on a mammoth
world tour, taking time out in May to attend the
Montreux pop festival. The first concert, in Rio
was at the biggest football stadium in the world,
filled before a 200,000 capacity audience. The
singer reflected that it was one of his most
extraordinary experiences.
While in South America Sting visited a native tribe
seldom visited by outsiders in view of their
reclusive nature. On the *Michael Aspel Show* Sting
commented that their lifestyle was the nearest
thing to paradise he'd ever known, living as they
did in perfect harmony with their environment.
They even performed a fertility dance for him.
"As if I need it," he joked. He performed the song
'Fragile' to the tribe with his percussionist backing
on an array of pots and pans he'd found in
neighbouring huts. In tribute afterwards a Pit
Viper was painted on his chest in red dye. That
night he and Trudi slept on tree hammocks, but
were woken deep into the evening as a real Pit
Viper, a snake capable of leaping 10 feet and killing
in seconds, was spotted only yards away. Luckily
the two guards who stood beside the couple
managed to kill the snake. Their explanation was
that as Sting wore its markings the reptile had
come to pay homage. The real reason was that the
snake was cold and wanted a warm body to
snuggle up to.

Also appearing on the *Michael Aspel Show* was Dustin Hoffman, whose first composition, 'Shoot The Breeze', was sung by Sting with the actor accompanying him on piano.

In South America Sting also became aware of the problem of the rain forests, where an area the size of a football pitch is being destroyed every day. What shook him was flying over an arid desert which had once been a thriving jungle. As a protest against this escalating madness he took part in a musical at The Kennedy Centre in Washington with 200 Blackburn school children. He was the narrator for one night only and also hoped to make a documentary with the BBC about the problem. Sting's tour came to Britain in December 1987 with the main dates at Wembley Arena. On December 20 he played an extra night with proceeds going to SANE, 'Schizophrenia – A National Emergency'.

CHAPTER FIFTEEN

AMNESTY INTERNATIONAL — HUMAN RIGHTS NOW TOUR

"For the first time we have been able to have an effect on the torture or wrongful imprisonment of people just by making records, all you do is embarrass governments, it's a wonderful way of achieving things."

ON **S**EPTEMBER 2 Sting performed at London's Wembley Stadium at the start of the Amnesty International 19-city Human Rights Now World Tour, on the same bill as Bruce Springsteen, Peter Gabriel, Tracy Chapman and Youssou N'Dour.

He first became aware of the activities of Amnesty when he appeared in one of their charity shows, *The Secret Policeman's Other Ball* in 1981. He later took part, along with U2 and Peter Gabriel, in The Conspiracy Of Hope Tour, a fortnight of American concerts in 1986 covering six cities and raising over two-and-a-half million dollars. Asked if he would do it all again Sting agreed on the spot, and he was the second star after Gabriel to sign up for the tour. They both attended the press conference on December 9, 1987 in São Paulo, Brazil, to announce the event. "I believe Amnesty is one of the most civilised organisations in the history of the world," Sting later declared.

This tour differed greatly from its predecessor. It was on a much grander scale, stretching to all corners of the globe except Australasia, an astonishing feat considering the logistical problems

and the delicate political message the tour
endorsed. The aim of the concerts was simple: to
tour the developed Western countries and raise
people's consciousness over the human rights issue
and the injustices that occur in other countries, and
also play in areas like South America, where rights
were so badly abused. The concerts were lent
additional purpose as 1988 was the anniversary
of the Declaration Of Human Rights.
The tour began in Europe, opening in a typically
wet London where Sting, the penultimate act,
opened with 'King Of Pain' and dedicated 'If You
Love Somebody' to all the children in South
African jails. Two shows followed at the Palais
Omnisports Bercy, a small indoor arena in Paris.
Sting performed Jacques Brel's 'Ne Me Quitte Pas'
('Don't Leave Me') and duetted with Springsteen
on 'The River'.
One of the more memorable features of the tour
were the press conferences held the morning before
each performance. In Budapest Sting was reminded
by a reporter that he once said that he'd been a
Marxist as a teenager. "My views have changed a
lot since I was 15," he replied. "They are very
complex and sometimes change daily. I now consider
myself a political party of one." 80,000 fans paid
the equivalent of a pound to see what was deemed
the largest rock event in Hungary's history.
The European leg of the tour closed in Barcelona
where Sting spoke to the audience in Spanish,
denouncing the government of Chile before
singing 'They Dance Alone'. "I think people are
going to talk about this tour for years to come," he
ventured during his stay. "It's going to be viewed
as an historical event." After stopping in San José
the tour moved to Canada for two shows in the
middle of September. In Montreal Sting met a
group of Chilean refugee women who presented
him with a poncho made by the relatives of the

'disappeared' as a gift of thanks for his song 'They Dance Alone' which became an anthem for those fighting the oppressive government, and even played a small role in the campaign to defeat the country's leader General Pinochet in the recent plebiscite.

On September 19 the tour hit America where the best of three shows was in Los Angeles. Sting joined Gabriel on his song 'Games Without Frontiers' and U2's Bono made a guest appearance at the finale. Prior engagements meant that Sting missed the next two concerts in Oakland, California and Tokyo, but rejoined the tour on September 30 for a performance in Delhi. In Athens he celebrated his 37th birthday in a traditional Greek restaurant.

The next port of call was Zimbabwe, close to the borders of South Africa, a fact not lost on the performers who responded by giving the 20,000 South Africans who crossed the border an unforgettable night. In Abidjan, Côte d'Ivoire, Sting appeared first on the bill for the only time and gave possibly his finest performance of the tour.

The last three concerts took place in South America. Here Sting received star treatment having toured before with The Police and then solo in 1987. He feels strongly about the troubles facing the continent, especially the abuse of native Indians in Brazil and the demolition of the Amazon rain forests. It was during his 1987 visit that he realised the severity of the problem. "I was in a plane flying over what looked like a desert. It was red and dusty with a few tree stumps. A Belgian film maker I was travelling with told me that 15 years before it had all been forest."

At the obligatory pre-show press conference Sting raised the subject and achieved substantial results when, before the show, Brazilian officials

announced new reforms to their forest policy.
Hardly convinced, Sting pressed the issue home
on-stage that evening when he was joined by Raoni,
the chief of the Indians he had befriended, and sang
a traditional song 'Tama Tama Teo Ay', his face
covered in war paint. It was a haunting spectacle.
The most heart-rending moment of the six-week
tour was reserved for the penultimate concert the
following night in Mendoza, Argentina, a country
separated from Chile only by the natural boundary
of the Andes peaks. A mere five days before the
show, 15,000 Chileans had travelled to the city to
celebrate a plebiscite that had prevented General
Pinochet from remaining in power until 1997, thus
releasing the people from 15 years of brutal
military rule, although oppression and abuse of
human rights has not been eliminated.

At the end of Sting's set he invited 25 mothers,
sisters and daughters of the 'disappeared' on-stage
with him during 'They Dance Alone'. Standing
solemnly they held pictures of their lost loved ones
and the song achieved a new level of poignancy.
Sting was joined by Gabriel and together they
danced with each woman in turn. Some broke
down in tears while others simply hugged
Sting, speaking volumes of thanks in one brief
emotion filled gesture. It was a stirring moment,
the highpoint of the tour and arguably of
Sting's career.

CHAPTER SIXTEEN

STORMY MONDAY — JULIA AND JULIA

"I've made 10 films, some good, some bad, some indifferent. But I don't want to be a movie star."

THERE **S A SCENE** in *Stormy Monday* which ought to convince even the toughest critic that Sting has developed into a credible British screen actor. It is the sequence in which he observes one of his employees casually breaking the forearm of a mobster. It's gritty and nasty, and Sting totally controls the scene, judging his performance carefully throughout. "But I hate all this Stallone shit. I hate seeing actors with guns, there they are on every movie poster looking like complete dickheads. I've been offered those films and I won't do them. That scene in *Stormy Monday* involved a gun and I wouldn't do it unless my character was allowed to say how much he hated them."

The plot of *Stormy Monday* revolves around Cosmo, a ruthless businessman who arrives in Newcastle from the USA during the town's America week, a celebration of Anglo-American trade. With the council's blessing he intends to buy and redevelop the quay, the area's equivalent of London's docklands. But one property, a jazz den called the Key Club run by the tough Finney (Sting), eludes him. How Cosmo sets about acquiring the club, his subsequent battle with Finney and the effect of the confrontation on sections of the town's inhabitants, provides the narrative thread of the film.

The idea for the movie originated in 1984 when director Mike Figgis and producer Nigel Stafford-

Clark collaborated on *The House*, an unusual film drama for Channel Four. Figgis mentioned then that he'd like to tackle a 'Newcastle' thriller. A year later a treatment was submitted to Channel Four who agreed to put up some of the money, but most of the finance came from British Screen and the American company, Atlantic Entertainment who have since assisted other British productions including *Wish You Were Here* and *A World Apart*, a film that won 13-year-old Jodhi May the best actress award, presented by Sting, at the Cannes film festival. But *Stormy Monday* was the first British film to benefit from Atlantic's benevolence.

As Finney, Sting is self-assured and positive. Talking in the accent of his upbringing, he looked more at ease in the role than any he has so far played. His style of acting is certainly more akin to the traditions of British theatre than the techniques of American method actors. "I'm more interested in sub-text and thorough rehearsal," he says. "I don't like method acting, it's such a waste of energy. If someone is your enemy in the script, he doesn't have to be your enemy all day."

His fondness and sense of security during rehearsal was explored in an interview with *Time Out* in 1989. "Some people are more relaxed about the process of being on camera. I'm not. I like to be in control and well prepared, that's why I need good directors. The way I view acting is as a craft to learn, not something you are born with. Being once married to an actress, most of the people in the profession that I met came through the tradition of drama school and rep. That is what I want to do, I'm learning as I go. I'm not interested in exploding on to the screen, I do that somewhere else."

Since director Mike Figgis had lived in Newcastle for many years he was keen from the outset to win

Sting's involvement. He even flew to LA to persuade him to accept the part. The script for *Stormy Monday* had been sent to Sting in Malibu by his Hollywood agent whose innocent enquiry, "Have you heard of Newcastle?" was greeted with the frosty retort, "I'm from Newcastle you dick!" "Sting is the biggest revelation in the film," Figgis says. "The idea to cast him came to me out of the blue, originally we had been thinking of much older actors. I've always admired his low-key performance in *Plenty*. He was very receptive to the idea of doing a part set in Newcastle. In fact he recognised a lot of the local and musical references in the script." Sting actually knew Mike Figgis when the latter played trumpet in Bryan Ferry's band The Gas Board.

Sting talked about how he approached the role of Finney. "When I used to play jazz, I played in clubs like his one, and so my research was just to remember what these people did, how they talked, what they looked like. It was nice to go back to your home town and do something that is such a fantasy."

Stormy Monday was filmed entirely on location in Newcastle. "Even though there was a lot of publicity due to the fact that Sting was in the film, there was never a feeling that we had taken over the town," said producer Nigel Stafford-Clark. "They just let us get on with it." During the filming Sting made a nostalgic visit to the streets where he had lived and to St. Cuthbert's Grammar school. "It was the summer holidays so no one was around. I drove in through the gates and still got that feeling of horror in my gut. I couldn't believe it of myself, a grown man, successful, four children and I'm still a kid in short trousers, terrified of the teachers. It's strange how those old feelings of dread can come back to haunt you."

Despite good performances, particularly from
Sting, the film fails on many of the levels it seeks to
attain. It isn't cinematic enough to hold the
attention, and looks, like most British films of this
type and period, too made for television, and when
stretched to accommodate the wide screen the
holes are glaringly obvious.

Released in America in the first week of May 1988,
reviews were unfavourable. *Premiere* magazine
singled out Melanie Griffith, who plays the woman
caught up in the cross fire of the men, for praise,
but said that the film's only enduring interest was
its portrayal of a working class England throttled
by American power playing. *Variety* commented:
"An attempt to come up with another British
Mona Lisa fails here. Sting's acting is fine, but like
Mick Jagger he can't seem to find a suitable film
project for his talents." *Film Review* however
called it, "enjoyable, strong-arm stuff." *Stormy
Monday* was well received in Cannes however,
with Sting and Melanie Griffith there in person
to promote the film. It opened in Britain on
January 20, 1989.

Sting's second film of 1988, *Julia And Julia*, teamed
him up, after Meryl Streep, with America's other
great modern actress Kathleen Turner. The film,
made in Italy, was the first feature to be shot in
high-definition video and then transferred to film,
supposedly giving the picture more clarity and
depth. This process leads to little atmosphere being
created on screen and makes the whole production
resemble a European television soap opera.

Released on February 5, 1988, it fared badly and
was not shown theatrically in Britain, instead
coming straight out on video in November
the same year.

However disappointing these two films were,
Sting escaped them relatively unscathed. His
performances in them both were his most sustained

and believable to date. He improves as he
progresses; if the right part comes along we may
well see a performance to equal that of his obvious
musical talents.

From the outset Sting has presented the public
with a fixed image but throughout his subsequent
career he has offered occasional glimpses and clues
as to his true self. He has confessed to creating
Sting to protect his other self – Gordon Sumner –
from the star system. "It's Sting who's the
superstar, he has all the fans, not me," he
acknowledged in *You* magazine in 1985. In a
variety of revealing quotes over the years he has
analysed the image he consciously created. "It
changes very subtly," he told *Films And Filming* in
1982. "But it remains a fairly impregnable image.
It's been very successful." He told *No.1* magazine:
"The Sting persona is a protective device and I
work hard at it." And for a 1985 *Woman* interview
. . . "I'm very satisfied that people are fairly
confused about what I am. As soon as they're sure
you're finished. So I just keep avoiding the issue.
The confusion is great, it's freedom."

He has admitted that at the age of seven he
destroyed every picture ever taken of himself.
It seems that from the very beginning he
began experimenting with creating a public,
rootless persona.

Coming to terms with an image that was neither
good nor bad has led Sting to purposely court film
roles that were closely linked to his own self,
characters who possessed both light and dark
personalities. *Brimstone And Treacle* and *The
Bride* were extensions and forays into his own
psyche, all very good therapy. In 1982, though,
both sides clashed, good merged with evil and
there occurred a period that Sting now refers
to as 'the fall'.

"At first I was the golden boy of pop, everything was wonderful. Then suddenly a total dive and all the press coverage was about drug taking, philandering and being a complete maniac." The pit of depression that almost engulfed Sting, a period brought on by his marriage break-up, the Virgin court case and general media hostility, was in his own words, "fairly terrifying." But it was useful as it ultimately allowed him to be what he wanted. "Now no one knows what to expect of me, whether I'm a decent bloke or an ego-maniac." Sting has often admitted to being completely addicted to success, so is it his other half, Gordon Sumner, who sometimes lets slip his wish for a normal life as in a *Record Mirror* interview in 1981. "I think it would be nice to have a nine-to-five job, go home, have tea and watch *Coronation Street*." On the *Michael Aspel Show* in early September 1988 he was asked if he thought he led a normal life. "I suppose so," he replied. "I live in Highgate, I go to the pub and the betting shop."

He has also been burdened with pop's sex symbol tag ever since The Police first made headlines. "It was imposed on me really. Every time *The Sun* prints a picture of me it's sexy Sting. I don't go round to people saying 'Hello I'm sexy Sting', it's not something I personally manufactured. The sex symbol thing is a bit of a joke, it got in the way of any serious issues we may have had. I just accepted it." Sting had always occupied the brightest part of the spotlight and therefore much of the public responsibility of the group rested on his shoulders. But to his credit he has managed to escape the pin-up circus to emerge in the late eighties as an internationally respected and popular artist.

But the literary references in his lyrics, the jazz influences and much flag waving for worthy causes have all led to accusations of pretentiousness. "I come in for a lot of flak on that score," he says.

"But I can live with it. I get letters from kids who read something because I referred to it on an album, a Shakespearean sonnet or something by Jung, or Koestler, or Nabokov's *Lolita*. I can't say I'm sorry, I think it's great."

But being an acknowledged serious rock star has its drawbacks as Sting described to *The Times* in 1986. "I've been asked to do outrageous things such as speak at the Oxford debate. Just because a person can make hit records doesn't mean they can do brain surgery or design an aircraft."

During the last few years Sting has become more publicly active concerning world issues. From venting early feelings on such topics as nuclear war and Ireland via 'Ghost In The Machine' and 'Synchronicity', he has in the last few years used his star status, like the best of his contemporaries, as a platform to speak to the world. His triumphs at *Live Aid*, the Mandela concert, the massive 1988 world Amnesty tour and his public misgivings over the destruction of South America's rain forests are proof of this. But again he has been attacked from sections of the press, this time for caring too much.

His acting career has progressed along similar lines, and he has been obliged to learn his craft in the glare of the public eye. Quite wisely his early film roles were short cameo appearances in home-grown movies like *Quadrophenia*. His first leading role was still within a British feature, thus protecting him from the critics if the progression failed. Instead he won rave notices, recognition and an assured Hollywood future. Since then a definite improvement in all of his cinema performances can be traced up to his most convincing role to date in *Stormy Monday*.

Along with David Bowie, Sting surely ranks as the most successful rock star turned film actor, and he shares with Bowie another trait, the art of projecting characters and public personas to hide the genuine self. Whatever Sting may have lacked in dramatic experience during his early movie excursions he made up for in genuine screen presence. Even in a film as flawed as *The Bride* his aura was undeniable, taking command of the action and demanding the viewer's attention. It is a unique natural talent that few esteemed actors even possess. This may be one of the reasons why so many rock stars are asked to appear in films, the reasoning being that if they can hold a live audience of thousands they should have few problems captivating cinema-goers.

Sting has now risen above merely being used as a pop star to lend novelty effect to an otherwise mediocre movie, and become a serious actor, respected among the film community. It is a great achievement and no less impressive than his success as a solo artist since the demise of The Police. Unlike any other rock star in history Sting has worked and excelled in all mediums: records, cinema, television, radio and now the stage. No other music performer to date can match such an impressive record. So what is left, Sting the novelist perhaps, he has already voiced an interest in writing a book, or maybe directing. As his past, varied career can testify, anything is possible. Asked by *NME* how he would like to be remembered he replied: "I'd like my children to remember me. I'd like the songs to survive. I'd just like to be remembered as someone reasonable, a reasonable bloke." He will be cherished as something more than that.

DISCOGRAPHY

POLICE 7″ SINGLES

Fall Out/Nothing Achieving
Illegal IL 001   May 1977
(reissued December 1979)

Roxanne/Peanuts
A&M AMS7348   April 1978
(reissued April 1979 in black and blue vinyl)

Can't Stand Losing You/Dead End Job
A&M AMS 7381   August 1978 (issued in black vinyl and blue
vinyl; reissued in June 1979 in black, dark blue, light blue,
green, yellow, red and white vinyls)

So Lonely/No Time This Time
A&M AMS 7402   October 1978
(reissued February 1980)

Message In A Bottle/Landlord
A&M AMS 7474   September 1979
(issued in black vinyl and green vinyl)

Walking On The Moon/Visions Of The Night
A&M AMS 7494   December 1979

Police Pack
(Six single pack comprising the five A&M singles above plus
Truth Hits Everybody/The Bed's Too Big Without You. All
with picture labels pressed on blue vinyl)
A&M AMPP 6001   May 1980

Don't Stand So Close To Me/Friends
A&M AMS 7564   September 1980
(initial copies in poster sleeve)

De Do Do Do De Da Da Da/A Sermon
A&M AMS 7578   December 1980

Invisible Sun/Shamelle
A&M AMS 8164   September 1981

Every Little Thing She Does Is Magic/Flexible Strategies
A&M AMS 8174   October 1981

Spirits In The Material World/Low Life
A&M AMS 8194   November 1981
(initial copies in poster sleeve)

Every Breath You Take/Murder By Numbers
*A&M AM 117   June 1983 (initial copies in gatefold picture
sleeve with an extra single Truth Hits Everything/Man In A
Suitcase; also issued as 7" picture disc)*

**Wrapped Around Your Finger/
Someone To Talk To**
*A&M AM 127   July 1983 (also issued as three different picture
discs, one for each group member)*

Synchronicity 2/Once Upon A Daydream
A&M AM 153   October 1983

King Of Pain/Tea In The Sahara
A&M AM 176   January 1984

**Don't Stand So Close To Me ('86 remix)/
Don't Stand So Close To Me (live)**
A&M AM 354   October 1986

Roxanne/Synchronicity
A&M AM 365   November 1986

POLICE 12" SINGLES

Roxanne/Peanuts
A&M AMS 7348   April 1978
(reissued as AMSP 7348 in April 1979)

Walking On The Moon/Visions Of The Night
A&M AMSP 7494   December 1979

**Wrapped Around Your Finger/Someone To Talk To/
Message In A Bottle/I Burn for You**
A&M AMX 127   July 1983

Synchronicity 2/Once Upon A Dream
A&M AMX 153   October 1983

King Of Pain/Tea In The Sahara
A&M AMX 176   January 1984

**Don't Stand So Close To Me ('86 remix)/
Don't Stand So Close To Me (live)**
A&M AMY 354   October 1986

Roxanne/Synchronicity
A&M AMY 365   November 1986

POLICE LPs

Outlandos D'Amour
Next To You/So Lonely/Hole In My Life/Roxanne/Peanuts/
Can't Stand Losing You/Truth Hits Everybody/Born In The
50s/Be My Girl Sally/Masoko Tango
A&M AMLH 68502   October 1978
(also issued as AMLN 68502 on blue vinyl)

Reggatta De Blanc
Message In A Bottle/Reggatta De Blanc/It's Alright For You/
Bring On The Night/Deathwish/Walking On The Moon/On
Any Other Day/The Bed's Too Big Without You/Contact/
Does Everybody Stare/No Time This Time
A&M AMLH 64792   October 1979
(also issued as two 10" LPs in set)

Zenyatta Mondatta
Don't Stand So Close To Me/Driven To Tears/When The
World Is Running Down/Canary In A Coal Mine/Voices
Inside My Head/Bombs Away/De Do Do Do De Da Da Da/
Behind My Camel/Man In A Suitcase/Shadows In The Rain/
The Other Way Of Stopping
A&M AMLH 64831   October 1980

Ghost In The Machine
Spirits In The Material World/Every Little Thing She Does Is
Magic/Invisible Sun/Hungry For You/Demolition Man/Too
Much Information/Rehumanise Yourself/One World (Not
Three)/Omega Man/Secret Journey/Darkness
A&M AMLK 63730   September 1981

Synchronicity

Synchronicity 1/Walking In Your Footsteps/Oh My God/
Mother/Miss Gradenko/Synchronicity 2/
Every Breath You Take/King Of Pain/Wrapped Around Your
Finger/Tea In The Sahara
A&M AMLK 63735   June 1983
(issued in six different cover designs)

Every Breath You Take: The Singles

Roxanne/Can't Stand Losing You/Message In A Bottle/
Walking On The Moon/Don't Stand So Close To Me/De Do
Do Do De Da Da Da/Every Little Thing She Does Is Magic/
Invisible Sun/Spirits In The Material World/Every Breath You
Take/King Of Pain/Wrapped Around Your Finger
A&M EVERY 1   October 1986
(CD Version includes So Lonely)

**COMPILATIONS
INCLUDING POLICE
TRACKS**

Propaganda

Includes live versions of Landlord and Can't Get Next To
You
A&M AMLE 64782   September 1979

Urgh! A Music War

Includes live version of Driven To Tears
A&M AMLX 64692   August 1981

Brimstone And Treacle

Includes How Stupid Mr Bates, I Burn For You and A Kind
Of Loving
A&M AMLH 64915   September 1982

21 Years Of Alternative Radio One

Includes live version of Can't Stand Losing You
Strange Fruit SFRLP 200   October 1988

STING 7″ SINGLES

Spread A Little Happiness/Only You
A&M AMS 8242   August 1982

If You Love Somebody Set Them Free/
Another Day
A&M AM 258   May 1985

Love Is The Seventh Wave/Consider Me Gone
A&M AM 272   August 1985

Fortress Around Your Heart/
Shadows In The Dark
A&M AM 286   September 1985

Russians/Gabriel's Message
A&M AM 292   November 1985

Moon Over Bourbon Street/Mack The Knife
A&M AM 305   February 1986

We'll Be Together/Conversations With A Dog
A&M AM 410   October 1987

Englishman In New York/Ghost In The Street
A&M AM 431   February 1988

Fragile/Fragile (version)
A&M AM 439   April 1988

They Dance Alone/Ellas Dansan Solas
A&M AM 458   September 1988

STING 12″ SINGLES   If You Love Somebody Set Them Free (torch song mix)/If You Love Somebody Set Them Free (Jellybean mix)/If You Love Somebody Set Them Free (LP version)/Another Day
A&M AMY 258   June 1985

Love Is The Seventh Wave/Consider Me Gone/Love Is The Seventh Wave (live)
A&M AMY 272   August 1985

Fortress Around Your Heart/
Shadows In The Dark
A&M AMY 286   September 1985

Russians/Gabriel's Message/I Burn For You (live)
A&M AMY 292   November 1985

Moon Over Bourbon Street/Mack The Knife/Fortress Around Your Heart
A&M AMY 305   February 1986

We'll Be Together (extended version)/We'll Be Together (LP version)/Conversations With A Dog
A&M AMY 410   October 1987

Englishman In New York/Ghost In The Street/Bring On The Night (live)/When The World Is Running Down
A&M AMY 431   February 1988

Fragile/Fragil/Fragildad/Mariposa
A&M AMY 439   April 1988

They Dance Alone/Ellas Dansan Solas/
Si Estamos Juntos
A&M AMY 458   September 1988

STING CD SINGLES

We'll be Together (extended version)/We'll Be Together (LP version)/Conversations With A Dog
A&M AMCD 410   October 1987
(issued in 5" and 3" versions)

Englishman In New York/Ghost In The Street/Bring On The Night (live)/When The World Is Running down (live)
A&M AMCD 431   February 1988

Fragile/Fragil/Fragildad/Mariposa
A&M AMCD 439   April 1988

Someone To Watch Over Me/Englishman In New York/If You Love Somebody Set Them Free/Spread A Little Happiness
A&M AMCD 911   August 1988

They Dance Alone/Ellas Dansan Solas/
Si Estamos Juntos
A&M AMCD 458   September 1988

STING LPs

The Dream Of The Blue Turtles

If You Love Somebody Set Them Free/Love Is The Seventh
Wave/ We Work The Black Seam/Russians/Children's
Crusade/Shadows In The Rain/Consider Me Gone/The
Dream of The Blue Turtles/Moon Over Bourbon Street/
Fortress Around Your Heart
A&M DREAM 1   June 1985

Bring On The Night

Bring On The Night/Consider Me Gone/Low Life/We Work
The Black Seam/Driven To Tears/Dream Of The Blue
Turtles/Demolition Man/One World/Love Is The Seventh
Wave/Moon Over Bourbon Street/I Burn For You/Another
Day/Children's Crusade/Down So Long/Tea In The Sahara
A&M BRING 1   June 1986 (double LP)

Nothing Like The Sun

Lazarus Heart/Be Still My Beating Heart/Englishman In New
York/History Will Teach Us Nothing/They Dance Alone/
Fragile/We'll Be Together/Straight To My Heart/Rock
Steady/Sister Moon/Little Wing/The Secret Marriage
A&M AMA 6042   October 1987

**COMPILATIONS
INCLUDING STING
TRACKS**

The Secret Policeman's Other Ball – Music

Roxanne, Message In A Bottle and I Shall Be Released
Springtime Ha Ha 6004   March 1982

Brimstone And Treacle

Includes Brimstone And Treacle, Only You, Spread A Little
Happiness, You Know I Had The Strangest Dream and
Brimstone 2
A&M AMLH 64915   September 1982

Party Party

Includes Need Your Love So Bad and Tutti Frutti
A&M AMLH 68551   December 1982

Lost In The Stars
Includes Mack The Knife
A&M AMA 5105   November 1985

Conspiracy Of Hope
Includes Strange Fruit
Mercury MERH 99   November 1986

A Very Special Christmas
Includes Gabriel's Message
A&M AMA 3911   November 1987

STING WITH NEWCASTLE BIG BAND

The Newcastle Big Band
Impulse ISS NBB 106   1972 (LP)

STING WITH LAST EXIT

Whispering Voices/Evensong
Wudwink WUD 01   1975 (single)
First From Last Exit – 8-track tape

STING WITH NUCLEAR ACTORS

Nuclear Waste/Digital Love
Virgin NO NUKE 235   1978
(single; reissued in 1979 on Charly)
CYS 1058, and in 1980 on DB DBS 5)

STING WITH DIRE STRAITS

Money For Nothing
Vertigo DSTR 10   June 1985 (subsequently included on LPs
Brothers In Arms and Money for Nothing)

FILMOGRAPHY

QUADROPHENIA (1979)
Director: Franc Roddam
Producers: Roy Baird and Bill Curbishley
Exec Producers: Roger Daltrey, John Entwistle, Pete
Townshend and Keith Moon
Distributor: World Northal
Cast: Phil Daniels, Leslie Ash, Sting, Toyah Willcox
Certificate: 'X'
Running Time: 115 Mins

RADIO ON (1979)
Director: Christopher Petit
Producer: Keith Griffiths
Associate Prod: Wim Wenders
Distributor: British Film Institute
Cast: David Beams, Lisa Kreuzer, Sting
Certificate: 'X'
Running Time: 102 Mins

BRIMSTONE AND TREACLE (1982)
Director: Richard Loncraine
Producer: Kenneth Trodd
Distributor: Brent Walker
Cast: Sting, Denholm Elliot, Joan Plowright, Suzanna
Hamilton
Certificate: 'X'
Running Time: 87 Mins

THE SECRET POLICEMAN'S OTHER BALL (1982)
Director: Julien Temple
Producers: Martin Lewis, Peter Walker
Distributor: U.I.P.
Cast: John Cleese, Peter Cook, Sting, Michael Palin, Phil
Collins
Certificate: 'AA'
Running Time: 99 Mins

DUNE (1984)

Director: David Lynch
Producer: Raffaella De Laurentiis
Distributor: U.I.P.
Cast: Kyle MacLachlan, Francesca Annis, Max Von Sydow, Sting
Certificate: 'PG'
Running Time: 140 Mins (Original Theatrical Version)

THE BRIDE (1985)

Director: Franc Roddam
Producer: Victor Drai
Distributor: Columbia-EMI-Warner
Cast: Sting, Jennifer Beals, David Rappaport, Clancy Brown, Geraldine Page
Certificate: '15'
Running Time: 118 Mins

PLENTY (1985)

Director: Fred Schepisi
Producers: Edward R. Pressman and Joseph Papp
Distributor: Columbia-EMI-Warner
Cast: Meryl Streep, Charles Dance, Tracey Ullman, John Gielgud, Sting
Certificate: '15'
Running Time: 124 Mins

BRING ON THE NIGHT (1985)

Director: Michael Apted
Producer: David Manson
Distributor: Miracle
Cast: Sting
Certificate: '15'
Running Time: 97 Mins

JULIA AND JULIA (1987)

Director: Peter Del Monte
Producer: RAI
Distributor: Cinecom Entertainment Group
Cast: Kathleen Turner, Gabriel Byrne, Sting
Certificate: '18'
Running Time: 98 Mins

STORMY MONDAY (1988)
Director: Mike Figgis
Producer: Nigel Stafford-Clark
Distributor: Atlantic Entertainment
Cast: Melanie Griffith, Tommy Lee Jones, Sting
Certificate: '15'
Running Time: 93 Mins

THE ADVENTURES OF BARON MUNCHAUSEN (1988)
Director: Terry Gilliam
Producer: Thomas Schuhly
Distributor: Columbia-Tri-star
Cast: John Neville, Oliver Reed, Robin Williams, Eric Idle, Sting
Certificate: PG
Running Time: 126 Mins

TELEVISION AND RADIO PRODUCTIONS

ARTEMIS '81 (1981)
Director: Alaistair Reid
Producer: David Rose
Story by: David Rudkin
Cast: Hywel Bennett, Sting
Broadcast: Tuesday December 29, 1981. BBC 1 9-00 pm/12-05 am

TITUS GROAN (1984)
By Mervyn Peake
Dramatised for radio by Brian Selby
Director: Glyn Dearman
Cast: Sting, Freddie Jones, David Warner, Eleanor Bron
Broadcast: Dec 10, 1984. Radio 4 8-15/9-45pm. Part One
Dec 17, 1984. Radio 4 8-15/9-45pm. Part Two

Omnibus Press
No.1 for Rock & Pop books.

Omnibus Press and Bobcat Books have published books on the
following rock and pop stars:

AC/DC ... Bryan Adams ... A-Ha ... The Alarm ... The Beatles ... Pat
Benatar ... Chuck Berry ... Big Country ... Black Sabbath ... Marc Bolan
... David Bowie ... Boy George & Culture Club ... Kate Bush ... Eric
Clapton ... The Clash ... Phil Collins ... Elvis Costello ... Crosby, Stills &
Nash ... The Cure ... Dead Or Alive ... Deep Purple ... Def Leppard ...
Depeche Mode ... The Doors ... Duran Duran ... Bob Dylan ...
Eurythmics ... Bryan Ferry & Roxy Music ... Fleetwood Mac ... Frankie
Goes To Hollywood ... Peter Gabriel ... Marvin Gaye ... Genesis ...
Jimi Hendrix ... Human League ... Billy Idol ... Julio Iglesias ... Michael
Jackson ... Mick Jagger ... The Jam ... Japan ... Billy Joel ... Elton John ...
Howard Jones ... Quincy Jones ... Journey ... Joy Division ... Judas Priest
... James Last ... Led Zeppelin ... John Lennon ... Madness ... Madonna
... Barry Manilow ... Marillion ... Bob Marley ... Paul McCartney ... Gary
Moore ... Jim Morrison ... Ozzy Osbourne ... Jimmy Page ... Pink Floyd
... The Police ... Elvis Presley ... The Pretenders ... Prince ... Queen ...
Quiet Riot ... Ratt ... Lou Reed ... Rolling Stones ... David Lee Roth ...
Rush ... The Sex Pistols ... Sigue Sigue Sputnik ... Simon & Garfunkel ...
Simple Minds ... Siouxie & The Banshees ... Slade ... The Smiths ...
Bruce Springsteen ... Status Quo ... Cat Stevens ... Sting ... Supertramp
... Talking Heads ... Tears For Fears ... Thompson Twins ... Pete
Townshend ... UB40 ... U2 ... Ultravox ... Van Halen ... The Velvet
Underground ... Wham! ... The Who ... Stevie Wonder ... Paul Young ...
Frank Zappa ... Z Z Top.

Omnibus and Bobcat titles on all the above are available from good
book, record and music shops. In case of difficulty, contact
Book Sales Ltd., Newmarket Road, Bury St. Edmunds, Suffolk IP33 3YB.